Sum Fun
Maths Assessment

Years 5–6
Maths Assessment Puzzles
for the
2014 Curriculum

Katherine Bennett

We hope you and your pupils enjoy solving the maths puzzles in this book. Brilliant Publications publishes other books for maths and maths problems. To find out more details on any of the titles listed below, please log onto our website: www.brilliantpublications.co.uk.

Maths Problem Solving Year 1   978-1-903853-74-0
Maths Problem Solving Year 2   978-1-903853-75-7
Maths Problem Solving Year 3   978-1-903853-76-4
Maths Problem Solving Year 4   978-1-903853-77-1
Maths Problem Solving Year 5   978-1-903853-78-8
Maths Problem Solving Year 6   978-1-903853-79-5

Maths Problems and Investigations 5–7 year olds   978-0-85747-626-5
Maths Problems and Investigations 7–9 year olds   978-0-85747-627-2
Maths Problems and Investigations 9–11 year olds   978-0-85747-628-9

The Mighty Multiples Times Table Challenge   978-0-85747-629-6

Published by Brilliant Publications
Unit 10
Sparrow Hall Farm
Edlesborough
Dunstable
Bedfordshire
LU6 2ES, UK

E-mail:
   info@brilliantpublications.co.uk
Website:
   www.brilliantpublications.co.uk
Tel:01525 222292

The name Brilliant Publications and the logo are registered trademarks.

Written by Katherine Bennett
Illustrated by Kerry Ingham
Front cover illustration by Kerry Ingham

© Text: Katherine Bennett 2014
© Design: Brilliant Publications 2014

Printed ISBN 978-1-78317-085-2
E-book ISBN 978-1-78317-090-6

First printed and published in the UK in 2014

Contents

Introduction

The aim of the 'Sum Fun' series is to enable teachers to gather evidence and assess children's learning in maths.

Linked to year group objectives from the new September 2014 curriculum, each fun activity sheet requires pupils to use their mathematical skills to solve a series of questions. They must then use the answers to 'crack the code' and find the solutions to silly jokes, puns and riddles. The activities use Assessment for Learning techniques such as child friendly 'I can...' statements at the top of each sheet so that pupils can be clear about the learning objective, and they also encourage self-assessment because if a solution doesn't make sense, pupils will need to spot and correct their mistakes. Quick reference answer pages are provided for the teacher at the back of the book, or to enable pupils to self-mark. There are several sheets per objective so that each one can be tested at different points in the year if necessary, without repetition of the same questions and jokes. This could be at the end of a unit of work, or as a one-off assessment task. The assessment checklist on pages 98–99 will help you to keep track of children's progress.

The activities are in a fun format that children soon become familiar with and look forward to solving, promoting high levels of pupil engagement. Children are motivated by the fun element of the jokes and will compete to be the first to get the answer!

As well as an assessment tool, the sheets can be used as independent tasks in everyday lessons. They are clearly linked to year group objectives from the new curriculum, providing an easy way of differentiating group or individual activities without any extra work for the class teacher! They make good whole class starter or plenary activities on an interactive whiteboard, or could just be used as fun 'time fillers'!

Place value and ordering (1)

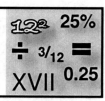

To solve the first joke, use place value to work out the value of the underlined digit and write the answer in the oval. Then use the grid to find the letter that goes with each answer and write it on the line. The first one is done for you!

30,000	300	300,000	5,000	800,000	3,000	900,000
M	A	B	O	K	W	R

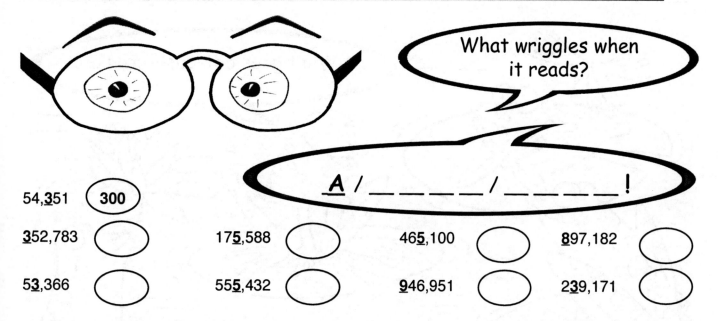

What wriggles when it reads?

A / ____ ____ / ____ ____ !

54,3<u>5</u>1 (300)

<u>3</u>52,783 ( )   17<u>5</u>,588 ( )   46<u>5</u>,100 ( )   <u>8</u>97,182 ( )

5<u>3</u>,366 ( )   55<u>5</u>,432 ( )   <u>9</u>46,951 ( )   2<u>3</u>9,171 ( )

This time, work out which is the biggest number and write it on the line. Use the grid to find the letter that goes with each answer.

865,039	125,608	865,093	354,354	125,806	124,086	354,543	865,309	354,345
N	L	S	T	U	R	G	B	O

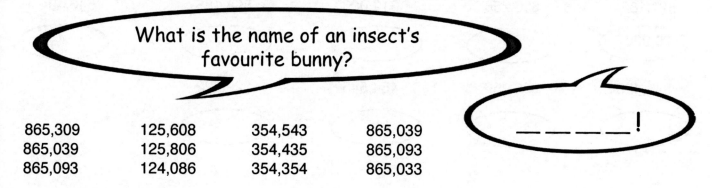

What is the name of an insect's favourite bunny?

____ ____ ____ ____ ____ !

865,309	125,608	354,543	865,039
865,039	125,806	354,435	865,093
865,093	124,086	354,354	865,033

____ ____ ____ ____ ____

Year 5 – Number and place value
- *Read, write, order and compare numbers to at least 1,000,000 and determine the value of each digit.*

Place value and ordering (2)

To solve the joke, use place value to work out the value of the underlined digit and write the answer in the oval. Then use the grid to find the letter that goes with each answer. The first one is done for you!

20,000	400	600,000	2,000	400,000	6,000	200,000	40,000
M	T	O	R	A	S	D	E

What goes dot-dash-croak?

M _ _ _ _ _ / _ _ _ _ !

8<u>2</u>7,182

<u>6</u>36,256

312,00<u>5</u>

89<u>6</u>,185

5<u>4</u>0,404

(20,000)

644,<u>4</u>28

<u>6</u>66,256

<u>4</u>54,545

<u>2</u>22,222

Year 5 – Number and place value
• *Read, write, order and compare numbers to at least 1,000,000 and determine the value of each digit.*

Place value and ordering (3)

Learning objectives
I know the value of each digit in numbers up to 1,000,000.
I can use place value to say which is the largest number.

To solve the joke, work out which is the largest number and write it on the line. Then use the grid to find the letter that goes with each answer. The first one is done for you!

658,123	981,981	443,158	658,321	443,185	659,112	981,891	444,518
K	G	T	E	H	R	F	M

982,981	443,518
O	I

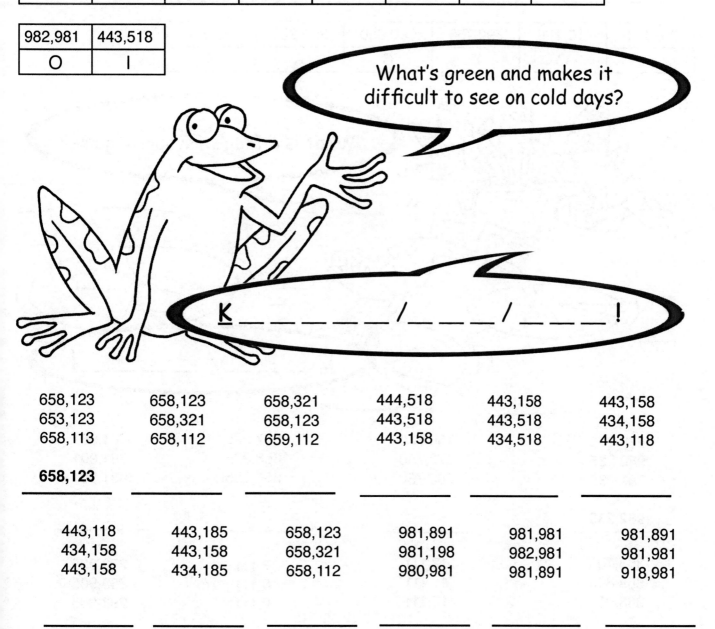

What's green and makes it difficult to see on cold days?

K____ ____ ____ ____ / ____ ____ ____ / ____ ____ ____ !

658,123	658,123	658,321	444,518	443,158	443,158
653,123	658,321	658,123	443,518	443,518	434,158
658,113	658,112	659,112	443,158	434,518	443,118

658,123
_____

443,118	443,185	658,123	981,891	981,981	981,891
434,158	443,158	658,321	981,198	982,981	981,981
443,158	434,185	658,112	980,981	981,891	918,981

Year 5 – Number and place value
* *Read, write, order and compare numbers to at least 1,000,000 and determine the value of each digit.*

Sequences in powers of 10 (1)

Learning objectives
I can count forwards and backwards in powers of 10, for example 100, 1000, 10,000.

123 25%
÷ 3/12 =
XVII 0.25

To solve the joke, work out the number that comes next and write it on the line. Then use the grid to find the letter that goes with each answer. The first one is done for you!

981,901	799,750	364,005	899,079	9,111	303,905
P	U	F	S	R	G

982,235	10,111	790,750	980,950	360,225	789,750
L	O	E	C	A	K

What is a frog's favourite game?

L _ _ _ _ / _ _ _ _ _ !

979,235	760,750	357,225	681,901
980,235	770,750	358,225	781,901
981,235	780,750	359,225	881,901
982,235	_____	_____	_____
363,705	12,111	7,111	273,905
363,805	11,111	8,111	283,905
363,905	10,111	9,111	293,905
_____	_____	_____	_____

Year 5 – Number and place value
- *Count forwards or backwards in steps of powers of 10 for any given number up to 1,000,000.*

Sequences in powers of 10 (2)

Learning objectives
I can count forwards and backwards in powers of 10, for example 100, 1000, 10,000.

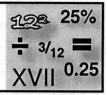

To solve the joke, work out the number that comes next and write it on the line. Then use the grid to find the letter that goes with each answer. The first one is done for you!

981,901	799,750	364,005	899,079	9,111	303,905
P	U	F	S	R	G

982,235	10,111	790,750	980,950	360,225	789,750
L	O	E	C	A	K

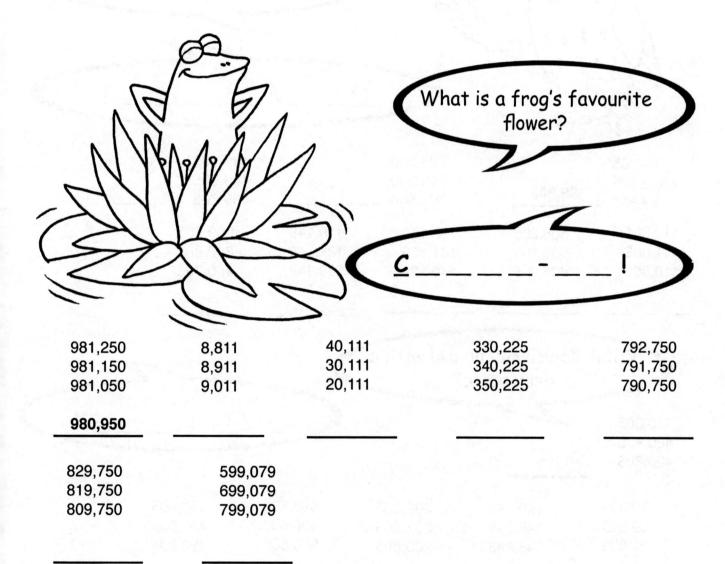

What is a frog's favourite flower?

C _ _ _ _ _ - _ _ !

981,250	8,811	40,111	330,225	792,750
981,150	8,911	30,111	340,225	791,750
981,050	9,011	20,111	350,225	790,750

980,950 _____   _____   _____   _____

829,750	599,079
819,750	699,079
809,750	799,079

_____   _____

Year 5 – Number and place value
* *Count forwards or backwards in steps of powers of 10 for any given number up to 1,000,000.*

Sequences in powers of 10 (3)

Learning objectives
I can count forwards and backwards in powers of 10, for example 100, 1000, 10,000.

122 25%
÷ 3/12 =
XVII 0.25

To solve the jokes, work out the number that comes next. Then use the grid to find the letter that goes with each answer. The first one is done for you!

605,905	139,139	199,805	149,149	690,500	500,805	489,805	109,805
E	B	O	R	W	A	L	G

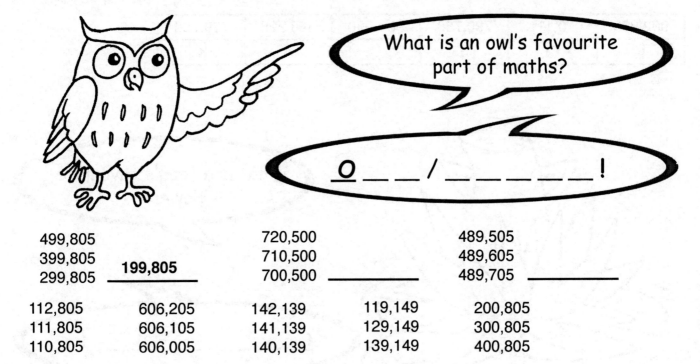

What is an owl's favourite part of maths?

O _ _ _ / _ _ _ _ _ _ !

499,805
399,805
299,805 **199,805** _____

720,500
710,500
700,500 _____

489,505
489,605
489,705 _____

112,805
111,805
110,805

606,205
606,105
606,005

142,139
141,139
140,139

119,149
129,149
139,149

200,805
300,805
400,805

___ ___ ___ ___

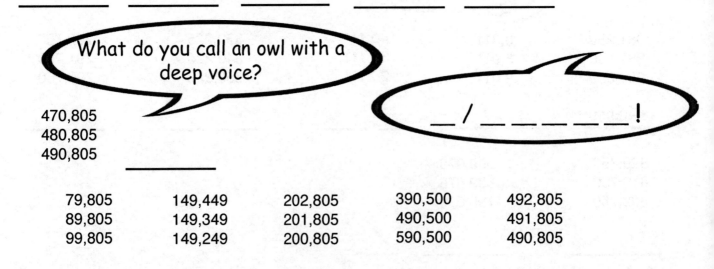

What do you call an owl with a deep voice?

_ / _ _ _ _ _ _ !

470,805
480,805
490,805
_____

79,805
89,805
99,805

149,449
149,349
149,249

202,805
201,805
200,805

390,500
490,500
590,500

492,805
491,805
490,805

___ ___ ___ ___ ___

Year 5 – Number and place value
• *Count forwards or backwards in steps of powers of 10 for any given number up to 1,000,000.*

Negative numbers (1)

Learning objectives
I can read negative numbers from temperature scales.
I can count forwards and backwards through zero.

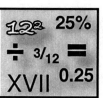

To solve the first joke, read the temperature from the scale and write the answer in the oval. Then use the grid to find the letter that goes with each answer. The first one is done for you!

-15	-10	-8	-1	-16	-2	-5	-6	-9	-4
C	S	H	A	E	O	P	D	L	I

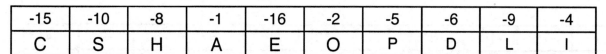

Where do baby fish go every morning?

P _ _ _ _ _ _ _ /
_ _ _ _ _ _ _ _ !

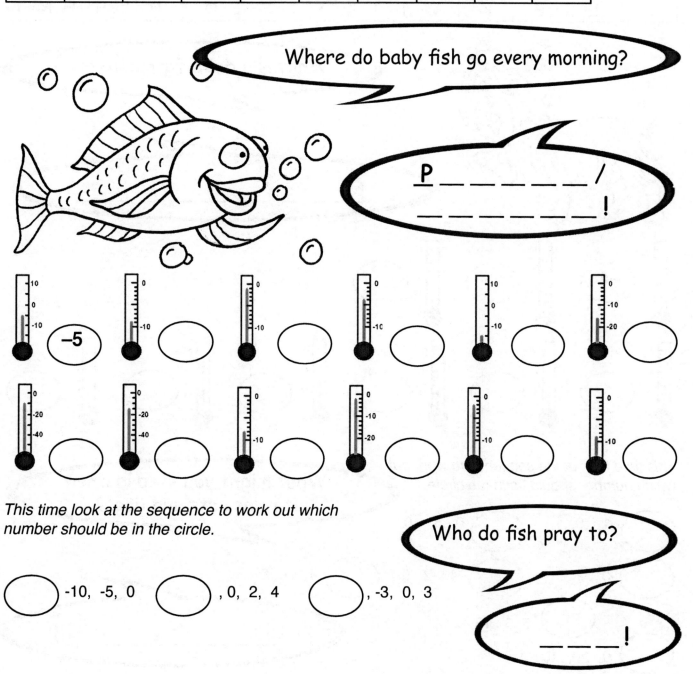

This time look at the sequence to work out which number should be in the circle.

( ) -10, -5, 0   ( ) , 0, 2, 4   ( ) , -3, 0, 3

Who do fish pray to?

_ _ _ _ !

Year 5 – Number and place value
- *Interpret negative numbers in context, count forwards and backwards with positive and negative whole numbers, including through zero.*

Negative numbers (2)

Learning objectives
I can read negative numbers from temperature scales.
I can count forwards and backwards through zero.

122 25%
÷ 3/12 =
XVII 0.25

To solve the first joke, read the temperature from the scale and write the answer in the oval. Then use the grid to find the letter that goes with each answer and write it on the line. The first one is done for you!

-20	-7	-15	-10	-8	-1	-16	-2	-5	-6	-9	-4
S	L	E	K	W	I	Y	P	O	D	R	N

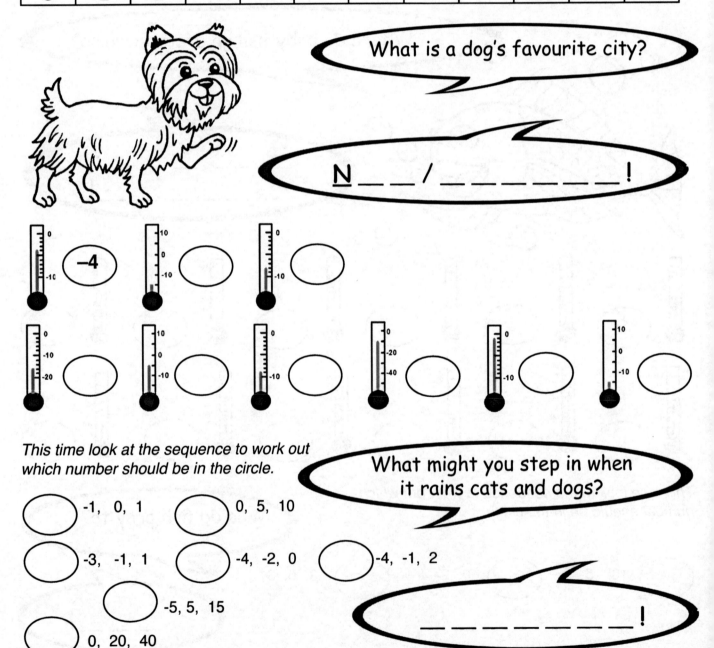

What is a dog's favourite city?

N _ _ _ / _ _ _ _ _ _ _ !

This time look at the sequence to work out which number should be in the circle.

-1, 0, 1

0, 5, 10

-3, -1, 1

-4, -2, 0

-4, -1, 2

-5, 5, 15

0, 20, 40

What might you step in when it rains cats and dogs?

_ _ _ _ _ _ _ !

Year 5 – Number and place value
• *Interpret negative numbers in context, count forwards and backwards with positive and negative whole numbers, including through zero.*

Rounding to 10, 100, 1000, 10,000 and 100,000 (1)

Learning objectives
I can round numbers to the nearest 10, 100, 1000, 10,000 or 100,000.

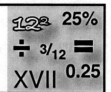

To solve the jokes, round each number according to the instructions and write it on the line. Then use the grid to find the letter that goes with each answer. The first one is done for you!

505,000	400,500	550,000	450,000	555,550	600,000	500,000	400,400
F	R	S	M	T	L	U	O

504,400	504,000
C	K

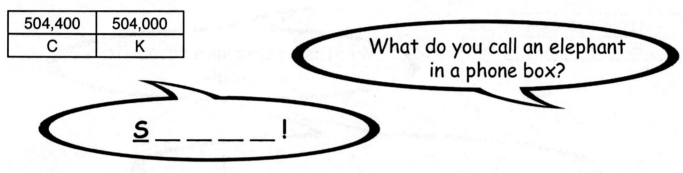

What do you call an elephant in a phone box?

S _ _ _ _ _ !

554,531 to the nearest 10,000 is

550,000

555,545 to the nearest 10 is

_____

458,150 to the nearest 100,000 is

_____

504,392 to the nearest 100 is

_____

504,199 to the nearest 1000 is

_____

561,222 to the nearest 100,000 is

_____

400,360 to the nearest 100 is

_____

What should you give an elephant who is about to be sick?

_ _ _ _ _ / _ _ _ /
_ _ _ _ _ !

555,554 to the nearest 10 is

_____

551,999 to the nearest 10,000 is

_____

400,449 to the nearest 100 is

_____

504,820 to the nearest 1000 is

_____

400,494 to the nearest 100 is

_____

400,391 to the nearest 100 is

_____

400,418 to the nearest 100 is

_____

454,500 to the nearest 10,000 is

_____

Year 5 – Number and place value
- *Round any number up to 1,000,000 to the nearest 10, 100, 1000, 10,000 and 100,000.*

Learning objectives
I can round numbers to the nearest 10, 100, 1000, 10,000 or 100,000.

123 25%
÷ 3/12 =
XVII 0.25

To solve the jokes, round each number according to the instructions and write it on the line. Then use the grid to find the letter that goes with each answer. The first one is done for you!

980,000	900,800	890,000	809,000	800,000	808,000	800,900	900,000
T	P	Q	A	U	S	I	L

908,000	890,890
E	K

What is a librarian's favourite vegetable?

Q _ _ _ _ _ _ / _ _ _ _ _ !

885,090 to the nearest 10,000 is
890,000

849,999 to the nearest 100,000 is
_____

800,851 to the nearest 100 is
_____

907,505 to the nearest 1000 is
_____

979,999 to the nearest 10 is
_____

900,751 to the nearest 100 is
_____

908,490 to the nearest 1000 is
_____

808,511 to the nearest 1000 is
_____

808,499 to the nearest 1000 is
_____

What is the worst vegetable to serve on a boat?

_ - _ _ _ _ _ !

809,188 to the nearest 1000 is
_____

851,111 to the nearest 100,000 is
_____

908,001 to the nearest 10 is
_____

908,009 to the nearest 1000 is
_____

890,894 to the nearest 10 is
_____

Year 5 – Number and place value
* *Round any number up to 1,000,000 to the nearest 10, 100, 1000, 10,000 and 100,000.*

Roman numerals (1)

Learning objectives
I can understand Roman numerals for numbers up to 1000.
I can recognise years written in Roman numerals.

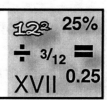

To solve the first joke, change the Roman numeral into a number and write the answer in the oval.
Then use the grid to find the letter that goes with each answer. The first one is done for you!

39	107	594	243	975	999	159	400
T	I	H	N	E	A	P	V

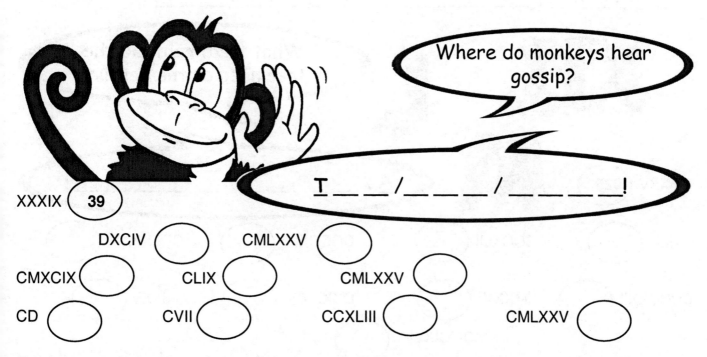

Where do monkeys hear gossip?

T _ _ _ / _ _ _ _ / _ _ _ _ _ !

XXXIX (39)

DXCIV ( )   CMLXXV ( )

CMXCIX ( )   CLIX ( )   CMLXXV ( )

CD ( )   CVII ( )   CCXLIII ( )   CMLXXV ( )

For the second joke, you need to work out what year is represented by the Roman numerals.

1949	1454	2011	1997	1456	1951	2009	1992
M	B	S	L	T	R	O	A

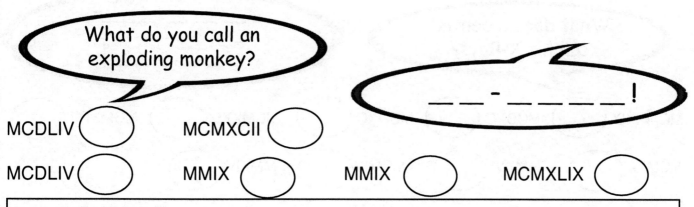

What do you call an exploding monkey?

_ _ - _ _ _ _ !

MCDLIV ( )   MCMXCII ( )

MCDLIV ( )   MMIX ( )   MMIX ( )   MCMXLIX ( )

Year 5 – Number and place value
• *Read Roman numerals to 1000 (M) and recognise years written in Roman numerals.*

Roman numerals (2)

To solve the joke, change the Roman numeral into a number and write the answer in the oval.
Then use the grid to find the letter that goes with each answer and write it on the line. The first one is done for you!

925	538	952	588	842	482	822
A	N	R	L	O	T	C

XII
L
M

What treatment did the tree need at the dentist.

CMXXV (925)

A / _____ / _____!

CMLII ( )   DCCCXLII ( )   DCCCXLII ( )   CDLXXXII ( )

DCCCXXII ( )   CMXXV ( )   DXXXVIII ( )   CMXXV ( )

DLXXXVIII ( )

For the second joke, you need to work out what year is represented by the Roman numerals.

2014	1929	1904	1490	2016	1992	1940
S	T	C	O	I	H	P

What does a dentist call his X-Rays?

_____ - _____!

MCMXXIX ( )   MCDXC ( )   MCDXC ( )   MCMXXIX ( )   MCMXCII ( )

MCMXL ( )   MMXVI ( )   MCMIV ( )   MMXIV ( )

Year 5 – Number and place value
* *Read Roman numerals to 1000 (M) and recognise years written in Roman numerals.*

Addition and subtraction (1)

Learning objectives
I can add two numbers with more than 4-digits.
I can subtract numbers with more than 4-digits.

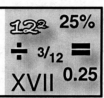

To solve the jokes, use a written method to find the answer and write it on the line. Then use the grid to find the letter that goes with each answer and write it in the speech bubble. The first one is done for you!

93,502	456,522	59,812	805,805	67,488	952,108	231,225	69,826	111,333
O	E	Y	I	G	A	L	N	P

What do you call a woman with one leg shorter than the other?

E_ _ - _ _ _ _ _!

125,311 + 331,211
= **456,522**

525,625 + 280,180
=

342,436 – 111,211
=

123,877 + 332,645
=

777,777 – 321,255
=

12,488 + 57,338
=

What do you call a dead parrot?

_ _ / _ _ _ _ _ _ - _ _ _ _!

554,983 + 397,125
=

235,268 – 123,935
=

11,351 + 82,151
=

113,113 + 118,112
=

93,243 – 33,431
=

105,623 – 38,135
=

368,254 – 274,752
=

35,272 + 34,554
=

Year 5 – Addition and subtraction
• *Add and subtract whole numbers with more than 4 digits, including using formal written methods (columnar addition and subtraction)*

Addition and subtraction (2)

Learning objectives
I can add two numbers with more than 4-digits.
I can subtract numbers with more than 4-digits.

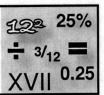

To solve the jokes, use a written method to find the answer and write it on the line. Then use the grid to find the letter that goes with each answer and write it in the speech bubble. The first one is done for you!

46,825	741,258	64,582	985,689	20,256	52,858	321,654	80,854	46,452	23,508
K	P	A	O	D	S	U	N	C	G

What are balloons scared of singing?

A / _ _ _ _ / _ _ _ _ _ !

25,368 + 39,214
= **64,582**

652852 + 88406
=

997,856 – 12167
=

852,649 – 111,391
=

13,689 + 39,169
=

11,587 + 974,102
=

91,368 – 10,514
=

15,204 + 8304
=

Which animal grows down instead of up?

_ / _ _ _ _ _ !

856 472 – 791 890
=

51,111 – 30,855
=

24,259 + 297,395
=

71,717 – 25,265
=

82,727 – 35,902
=

Year 5 – Addition and subtraction
• *Add and subtract whole numbers with more than 4 digits, including using formal written methods (columnar addition and subtraction)*

Prime numbers (1)

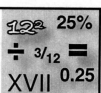

To solve the joke, work out which of the numbers in the list is the prime number. Then use the grid to find the letter that goes with each answer and write it on the line. The first one is done for you!

79	74	25	19	51	23	41	47	89	43	7	33	83
A	Q	B	R	C	S	D	T	E	U	F	V	G

57	37	31	27	63	67	87	11	91	59	53	73	21
W	I	H	J	Y	K	Z	L	X	M	N	O	P

What do you call a clever monster?

F _ _ _ _ _ /
_ _ _ _ _ _ _ _ _ !

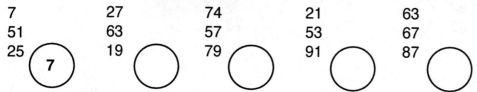

7	27	74	21	63
51	63	57	53	67
25	19	79	91	87
(7)	○	○	○	○

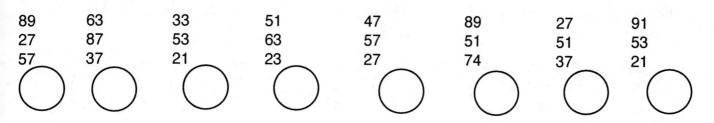

89	63	33	51	47	89	27	91
27	87	53	63	57	51	51	53
57	37	21	23	27	74	37	21
○	○	○	○	○	○	○	○

Year 5 – Multiplication and division
- Establish whether a number up to 100 is prime and recall prime numbers up to 19.

Prime numbers (2)

Learning objectives
I know the prime numbers up to 19.
I can work out whether numbers up to 100 are prime.

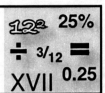

To solve the joke, work out which of the numbers in the list is the prime number. Then use the grid to find the letter that goes with each answer and write it on the line. The first one is done for you!

79	74	25	19	51	23	41	47	89	43	7	33	83
A	Q	B	R	C	S	D	T	E	U	F	V	G

57	37	31	27	63	67	87	11	91	59	53	73	21
W	I	H	J	Y	K	Z	L	X	M	N	O	P

What is a ghost's favourite Shakespeare play?

R _ _ _ _ _ / _ _ _ /
_ _ _ _ _ _ _ _ !

51 63 **(19)**	73 74 25 ( )	91 87 59 ( )	51 57 89 ( )	91 63 73 ( )

79 25 63 ( )	53 91 51 ( )	51 91 41 ( )	33 83 63 ( )	63 87 31 ( )

63 73 25 ( )	74 57 43 ( )	27 21 11 ( )	57 37 87 ( )	89 91 74 ( )	87 57 47 ( )

Year 5 – Multiplication and division
• *Establish whether a number up to 100 is prime and recall prime numbers up to 19.*

Prime numbers (3)

Learning objectives	
I know the prime numbers up to 19. I can work out whether numbers up to 100 are prime.	

To solve the joke, work out which of the numbers in the list is the prime number. Then use the grid to find the letter that goes with each answer and write it on the line. The first one is done for you!

37	53	65	7	14	59	89	24	5	61	79	84	29
A	Q	B	R	C	S	D	T	E	U	F	V	G

57	67	93	9	38	49	75	83	52	33	31	99	17
W	I	H	J	Y	K	Z	L	X	M	N	O	P

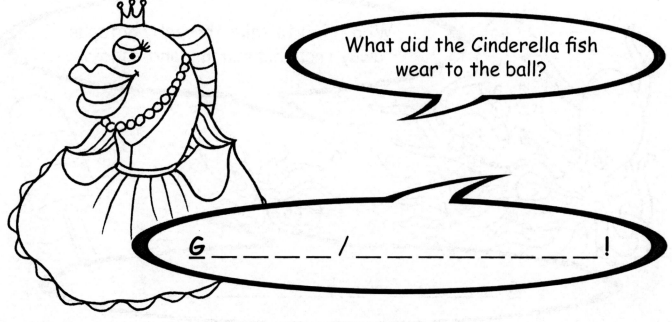

What did the Cinderella fish wear to the ball?

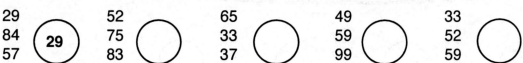

G _ _ _ _ _ _ / _ _ _ _ _ _ _ _ _ !

29 84 57	52 75 83	65 33 37	49 59 99	33 52 59
(29)	◯	◯	◯	◯

93 57 79	38 49 83	52 33 67	14 9 17	33 17 24	9 14 5	57 93 7	57 93 59
◯	◯	◯	◯	◯	◯	◯	◯

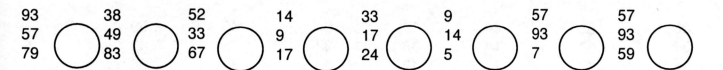

Year 5 – Multiplication and division
- *Establish whether a number up to 100 is prime and recall prime numbers up to 19.*

Prime numbers (4)

Learning objectives
I know the prime numbers up to 19.
I can work out whether numbers up to 100 are prime.

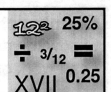

To solve the joke, work out which of the numbers in the list is the prime number. Then use the grid to find the letter that goes with each answer and write it on the line. The first one is done for you!

37	53	65	7	14	59	89	24	5	61	79	84	29
A	Q	B	R	C	S	D	T	E	U	F	V	G

57	67	93	9	38	49	75	83	52	33	31	99	17
W	I	H	J	Y	K	Z	L	X	M	N	O	P

Who tried to take the baby octopus away from his mummy and daddy?

<u>S</u> _ _ _ _ _ – _ _ _ _ _ _ _ _ !

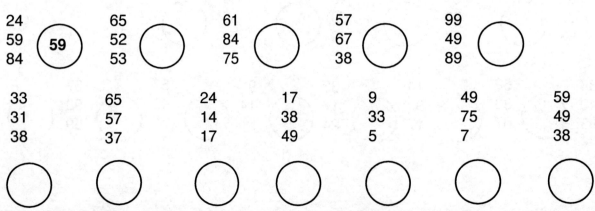

24
59 (59)
84

65
52
53

61
84
75

57
67
38

99
49
89

33
31
38

65
57
37

24
14
17

17
38
49

9
33
5

49
75
7

59
49
38

Long multiplication (1)

Learning objectives
I can use a written method to multiply numbers up to 4-digits by a 1 or a 2-digit number.

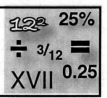

To solve the jokes, use a written method to calculate the answer. Then use the grid to find the letter that goes with each answer and write it on the line. The first one is done for you!

24,111	3176	4608	33,966	23,184	40,824	24,780	50,463	132,960
H	N	E	M	L	I	O	T	D

What do you say to a two-headed dinosaur?

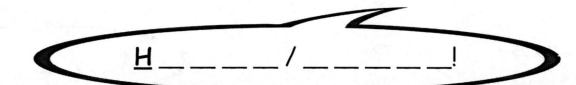

H _ _ _ _ _ / _ _ _ _ _ !

423 x 57 =
24111
_____

576 x 8 =
_____

336 x 69 =
_____

368 x 63 =
_____

3540 x 7 =
_____

513 x 47 =
_____

768 x 6 =
_____

552 x 42 =
_____

483 x 48 =
_____

1652 x 15 =
_____

What do you call an exploding dinosaur?

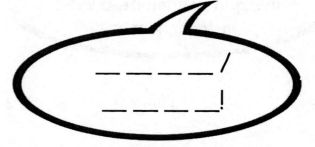

_ _ _ _ _ / _ _ _ _ !

4155 x 32 =
_____

648 x 63 =
_____

397 x 8 =
_____

2065 x 12 =
_____

3774 x 9 =
_____

486 x 84 =
_____

567 x 89 =
_____

1152 x 4 =
_____

Year 5 – Multiplication and division
*   *Multiply numbers up to 4 digits by a one- or two-digit number using a formal written method, including long multiplication for two-digit numbers.*

Long multiplication (2)

Learning objectives
I can use a written method to multiply numbers up to 4-digits by a 1
  or a 2-digit number.

25% ÷ 3/12 = XVII 0.25

To solve the jokes, use a written method to calculate the answer. Then use the grid to find the letter that goes with each answer and write it on the line. The first one is done for you!

25,784	7554	28,782	8346	29,667	35,216	31,524	30,510	32,562
G	H	S	A	L	N	I	E	V

What has to be broken before you can use it?

A __ / ____ !

321 x 26 =

8346

568 x 62 =

_____

5085 x 6 =

1172 x 22 =

293 x 88 =

Why can't a man living in London be buried in Manchester?

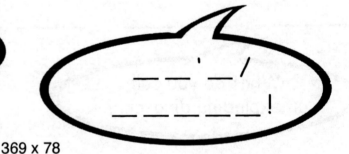

___ ___ ___ /
_____ !

1259 x 6
=

1695 x 18 =

369 x 78
=

214 x 39
=

319 x 93
=

5254 x 6
=

3618 x 9
=

6102 x 5
=

Year 5 – Multiplication and division
• *Multiply numbers up to 4 digits by a one- or two-digit number using a formal written method, including long multiplication for two-digit numbers.*

Short division (1)

Learning objectives
I can use a written method to divide a number with up to 4-digits
  by a 1-digit number.
If the answer is not a whole number, I can give it as a remainder,
  fraction or decimal.

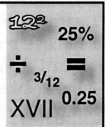

To solve the joke, use a written method to calculate the answer as a whole number, remainder, fraction or decimal. Then use the grid to find the letter that goes with each answer and write it on the line. The first one is done for you.

656.8	155 r 2	44½	456 r 1	357 r 4	96.25	32
H	A	E	B	R	S	M

269	856	87.5	431 r 2	37 r 6	724¾	352
O	I	L	T	N	C	G

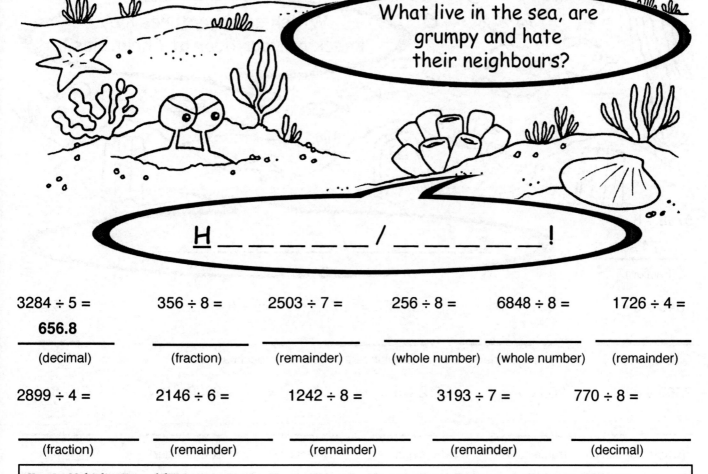

What live in the sea, are grumpy and hate their neighbours?

<u>H</u>_ _ _ _ _ _ / _ _ _ _ _ _ !

$3284 \div 5 =$
656.8

_____
(decimal)

$356 \div 8 =$

_____
(fraction)

$2503 \div 7 =$

_____
(remainder)

$256 \div 8 =$

_____
(whole number)

$6848 \div 8 =$

_____
(whole number)

$1726 \div 4 =$

_____
(remainder)

$2899 \div 4 =$

_____
(fraction)

$2146 \div 6 =$

_____
(remainder)

$1242 \div 8 =$

_____
(remainder)

$3193 \div 7 =$

_____
(remainder)

$770 \div 8 =$

_____
(decimal)

Year 5 – Multiplication and division
- *Divide numbers up to 4 digits by a one-digit number using the formal written method of short division and interpret remainders appropriately for the context.*

Short division (2)

Learning objectives
I can use a written method to divide a number with up to 4-digits
  by a 1-digit number.
If the answer is not a whole number, I can give it as a remainder,
  fraction or decimal.

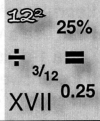

To solve the joke, use a written method to calculate the answer as a whole number, remainder, fraction or decimal. Then use the grid to find the letter that goes with each answer and write it on the line. The first one is done for you!

656.8	155 r 2	44½	456 r 1	357 r 4	96.25	32
H	A	E	B	R	S	M

269	856	87.5	431 r 2	37 r 6	724¾	352
O	I	L	T	N	C	G

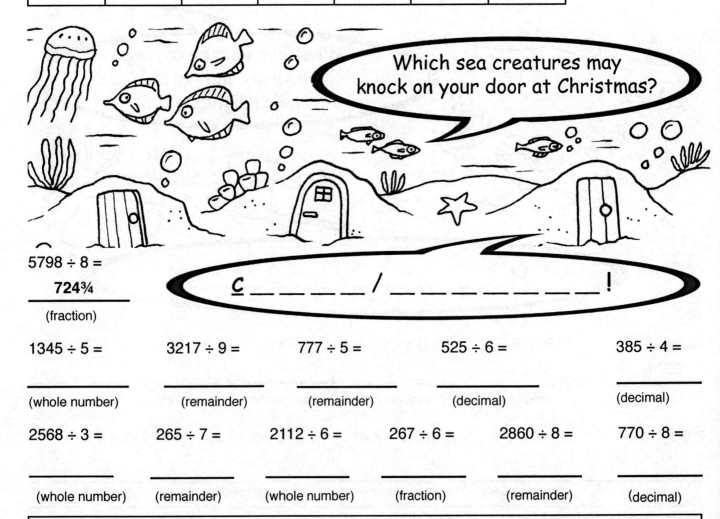

Which sea creatures may knock on your door at Christmas?

C _ _ _ _ _ / _ _ _ _ _ _ _ _ !

5798 ÷ 8 =
724¾
_____
(fraction)

1345 ÷ 5 =
_____
(whole number)

3217 ÷ 9 =
_____
(remainder)

777 ÷ 5 =
_____
(remainder)

525 ÷ 6 =
_____
(decimal)

385 ÷ 4 =
_____
(decimal)

2568 ÷ 3 =
_____
(whole number)

265 ÷ 7 =
_____
(remainder)

2112 ÷ 6 =
_____
(whole number)

267 ÷ 6 =
_____
(fraction)

2860 ÷ 8 =
_____
(remainder)

770 ÷ 8 =
_____
(decimal)

Year 5 – Multiplication and division
* *Divide numbers up to 4 digits by a one-digit number using the formal written method of short division and interpret remainders appropriately for the context.*

Short division (3)

Learning objectives
I can use a written method to divide a number with up to 4-digits
  by a 1-digit number.
If the answer is not a whole number, I can give it as a remainder,
  fraction or decimal.

12² 25%
÷ =
³/₁₂
XVII 0.25

To solve the joke, use a written method to calculate the answer as a whole number, remainder, fraction or decimal. Then use the grid to find the letter that goes with each answer and write it on the line. The first one is done for you!

622.5	236 r 3	89½	657	229 r 4	137 r 1	56¼	164.4	856
M	I	O	C	S	E	W	R	A

What is a cat's favourite dessert?

<u>M</u> __ __ __ __ / __ __ __ __ __ __ !

2490 ÷ 4 =

622.5
_____
(decimal)

1891 ÷ 8 =

_____
(remainder)

3942 ÷ 6 =

_____
(whole number)

549 ÷ 4 =

_____
(remainder

5913 ÷ 9 =

_____
(whole number)

822 ÷ 5 =

_____
(decimal)

1097 ÷ 8 =

_____
(remainder)

5992 ÷ 7 =

_____
(whole number)

4980 ÷ 8 =

_____
(decimal)

Year 5 – Multiplication and division
* *Divide numbers up to 4 digits by a one-digit number using the formal written method of short division and interpret remainders appropriately for the context.*

Short division (4)

Learning objectives
I can use a written method to divide a number with up to 4-digits
  by a 1-digit number.
If the answer is not a whole number, I can give it as a remainder,
  fraction or decimal.

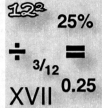

To solve the joke, use a written method to calculate the answer as a whole number, remainder, fraction or decimal. Then use the grid to find the letter that goes with each answer and write it on the line. The first one is done for you!

622.5	236 r 3	89½	657	229 r 4	137 r 1	56¼	164.4	856
M	I	O	C	S	E	W	R	A

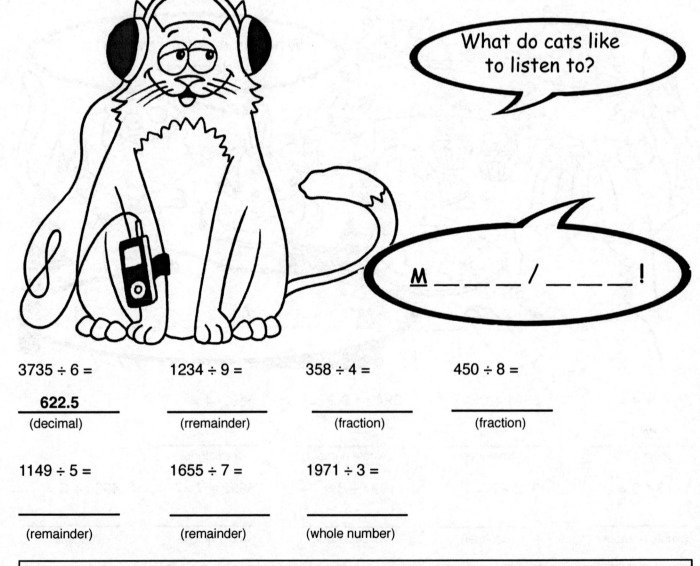

What do cats like to listen to?

M _ _ _ _ / _ _ _ _ !

3735 ÷ 6 =

622.5
(decimal)

1234 ÷ 9 =

_____
(rremainder)

358 ÷ 4 =

_____
(fraction)

450 ÷ 8 =

_____
(fraction)

1149 ÷ 5 =

_____
(remainder)

1655 ÷ 7 =

_____
(remainder)

1971 ÷ 3 =

_____
(whole number)

Year 5 – Multiplication and division
• *Divide numbers up to 4 digits by a one-digit number using the formal written method of short division and interpret remainders appropriately for the context.*

x and ÷ whole numbers and decimals by 10, 100 or 1000 (1)

Learning objectives	
I can multiply and divide whole numbers and decimals by 10, 100 or 1000.	12² 25% ÷ ³/₁₂ = XVII 0.25

To solve the joke, work out the answer by multiplying or dividing by 10, 100 or 1000. Then use the grid to find the letter that goes with each answer and write it on the line. The first one is done for you!.

0.28	14.6	0.035	3.5	0.59	590	350	146	1.46	2.8	2800	59
S	E	R	N	V	T	I	I	L	Y	A	O

What do you call a penguin in the desert?

V_ _ _ _ / _ _ _ _ !

5.9 ÷ 10 =

0.59

0.146 x 100 =

_____

35 ÷ 1000 =

_____

0.146 x 10 =

_____

1.46 x 100 =

_____

5.9 x 10 =

_____

28 ÷ 100 =

_____

0.59 x 1000 =

_____

Year 5 – Multiplication and division
* *Multiply and divide whole numbers and those involving decimals by 10, 100 and 1000.*

Learning objectives
I can multiply and divide whole numbers and decimals by 10, 100 or 1000.

123 25%
÷ 3/12 =
XVII 0.25

To solve the joke, work out the answer by multiplying or dividing by 10, 100 or 1000. Then use the grid to find the letter that goes with each answer and write it on the line. The first one is done for you!

0.28	14.6	0.035	3.5	0.59	590	350	146	1.46	2.8	2800	59
S	E	R	N	V	T	I	L	Y	A	G	O

Where do penguins go to the toilet?

I _ / _ _ / _ _ - _ _ _ !

3.5 x 100
=
350

3500 ÷ 1000

_____

280 ÷ 100 =

_____

3500 ÷ 1000

_____

0.35 x 1000 =

_____

2.8 x 1000 =

_____

1.46 x 100 =

_____

0.059 x 1000 =

_____

590 ÷ 10 =

_____

Year 5 – Multiplication and division
- *Multiply and divide whole numbers and those involving decimals by 10, 100 and 1000.*

x and ÷ whole numbers and decimals by 10, 100 or 1000 (3)

<table>
<tr><td>Learning objectives
I can multiply and divide whole numbers and decimals by 10, 100 or 1000.</td><td>123 25%
÷ 3/12 =
XVII 0.25</td></tr>
</table>

To solve the joke, work out the answer by multiplying or dividing by 10, 100 or 1000. Then use the grid to find the letter that goes with each answer and write it on the line. The first one is done for you!.

2.4	5.8	0.36	2400	470	360	580	3600	30.6	4700	240
H	S	N	M	E	F	I	A	L	B	K

What do you get from a cow that's had a bumpy ride?

<u>M</u> _ _ _ – _ _ _ _ _ !

24 x 100 =

2400

5800 ÷ 10 =

3060 ÷ 100 =

24000 ÷ 100 =

58 ÷ 10 =

24 ÷ 10 =

36 x 100 =

2400 ÷ 10 =

47 x 10 =

Year 5 – Multiplication and division
*   *Multiply and divide whole numbers and those involving decimals by 10, 100 and 1000.*

x and ÷ whole numbers and decimals by 10, 100 or 1000 (4)

Learning objectives
I can multiply and divide whole numbers and decimals by 10, 100 or 1000.

To solve the joke, work out the answer by multiplying or dividing by 10, 100 or 1000. Then use the grid to find the letter that goes with each answer and write it on the line. The first one is done for you!.

2.4	5.8	0.36	2400	470	360	580	3600	30.6	4700	240
H	S	N	M	E	F	I	A	L	B	K

What do you call a cow with two legs?

L _ _ _ / _ _ _ _ !

0.306 x 100 =

30.6
_____

0.47 x 1000 =

_____

36 x 100 =

_____

360 ÷ 1000 =

_____

4.7 x 1000 =

_____

4700 ÷ 10 =

_____

4.7 x 100 =

_____

0.36 x 1000 =

_____

_____   _____   _____   _____

Year 5 – Multiplication and division
- *Multiply and divide whole numbers and those involving decimals by 10, 100 and 1000.*

Square and cube numbers (1)

Learning objectives
I can recognise square numbers.
I can recognise cubed numbers.
I know the symbols for squared and cubed.

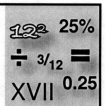

To solve the jokes, work out the answer and write it in the oval. Then use the grid to find the letter that goes with each answer and write it on the line.

8	81	64	16	9	27	1	36	125	25	49
R	W	T	I	H	N	E	D	L	O	S

What happens once in a year, twice in a week, but never in a day?

T _ _ / _ _ _ _ _ _ _ / _ !

$8^2 =$ (64) $3^2 =$ ( ) $1^2 =$ ( )

$5^3 =$ ( ) $1^3 =$ ( ) $4^3 =$ ( ) $8^2 =$ ( ) $1^2 =$ ( ) $2^3 =$ ( )

$1^3 =$ ( )

What invention allows you to see through walls?

_ _ _ _ /

_ _ _ _ _ _ _ !

$4^3 =$ (64) $3^2 =$ ( ) $1^2 =$ ( )

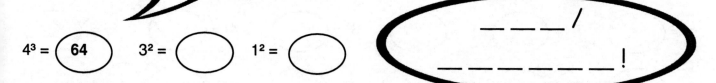

$9^2 =$ ( ) $4^2 =$ ( ) $3^3 =$ ( ) $6^2 =$ ( ) $5^2 =$ ( ) $9^2 =$ ( )

Year 5 – Multiplication and division
• *Recognise and use square numbers and cube numbers, and the notation for squared (^{2}) and cubed (^{3}).*

Square and cube numbers (2)

Learning objectives
I can recognise square numbers.
I can recognise cubed numbers.
I know the symbols for squared and cubed.

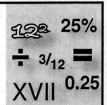

To solve the joke, work out the answer and write it in the oval. Then use the grid to find the letter that goes with each answer and write it on the line. The first one is done for you!

4	81	27	8	64	36	125	25	49	9
S	I	G	K	H	T	B	P	R	A

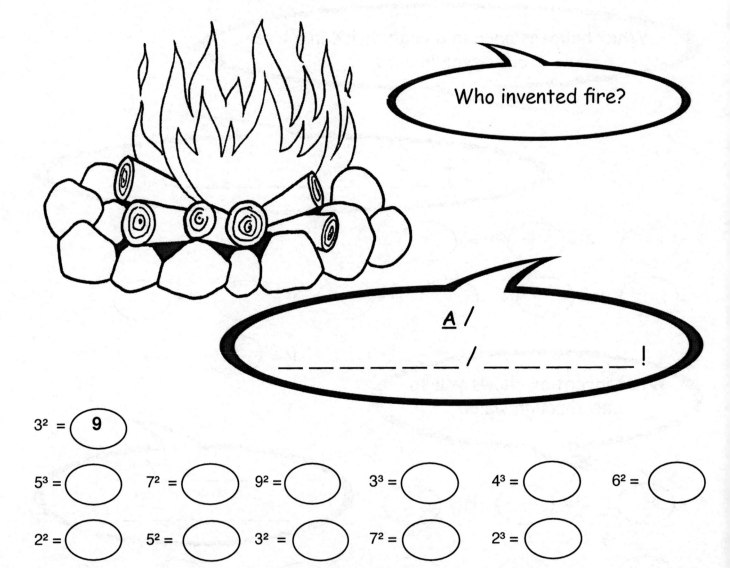

Who invented fire?

A / _____ / _____ !

$3^2 = \boxed{9}$

$5^3 = \bigcirc$ $7^2 = \bigcirc$ $9^2 = \bigcirc$ $3^3 = \bigcirc$ $4^3 = \bigcirc$ $6^2 = \bigcirc$

$2^2 = \bigcirc$ $5^2 = \bigcirc$ $3^2 = \bigcirc$ $7^2 = \bigcirc$ $2^3 = \bigcirc$

Year 5 – Multiplication and division
- *Recognise and use square numbers and cube numbers, and the notation for squared (^{2}) and cubed (^{3}).*

Square and cube numbers (3)

Learning objectives
I can recognise square numbers.
I can recognise cubed numbers.
I know the symbols for squared and cubed.

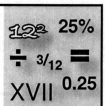

To solve the joke, work out the answer and write it in the oval. Then use the grid to find the letter that goes with each answer and write it on the line.

125	81	4	100	27	49	10	144	9	36	8	121	64	5
S	I	O	F	G	D	K	H	E	T	N	P	A	C

Where would you find giant snails?

$\underline{O}$ _ / _ /
_ _ _ _ _ ' _ / _ _ _ _ _ !

$2^2 =$ (4) $2^3 =$ ( ) $8^2 =$ ( )

$3^3 =$ ( ) $9^2 =$ ( ) $4^3 =$ ( ) $2^3 =$ ( ) $6^2 =$ ( ) $5^3 =$ ( )

$12^2 =$ ( ) $8^2 =$ ( ) $2^3 =$ ( ) $7^2 =$ ( )

Year 5 – Multiplication and division
* *Recognise and use square numbers and cube numbers, and the notation for squared (^{2}) and cubed (^{3}).*

Understanding the 'equals' sign (1)

<table>
<tr><td>**Learning objectives**
I can find the missing number to balance a calculation.</td><td>12² 25%
÷ 3/12 =
XVII 0.25</td></tr>
</table>

To solve the jokes, work out the answer and write it in the circle. Then use the grid to find the letter that goes with each answer and write it on the line. The first one is done for you!

13	100	55	25	60	32	90	75	47	10
W	C	S	I	A	R	M	T	N	O

What do you call a mouse who can pick up an elephant?

S _ _ !

$45 + (55) = 50 \times 2$ $75 + \bigcirc = 25 \times 4$ $\bigcirc \div 8 = 20 - 16$

Which superhero are mice scared of?

_ _ _ _ /
_ _ _ _ _ !

$\bigcirc - 30 = 35 \times 2$ $30 + \bigcirc = 10 \times 9$ $250 \div 10 = \bigcirc - 50$

$36 \div 2 = \bigcirc + 5$ $88 \div 8 = 110 \div \bigcirc$

$30 \div 3 = 100 - \bigcirc$ $880 \div 10 = 28 + \bigcirc$ $\bigcirc + 53 = 20 \times 5$

Year 5 – Multiplication and division
- *Solve problems involving addition, subtraction, multiplication and division and a combination of these, including understanding the meaning of the equals sign.*

Understanding the 'equals' sign (2)

Learning objectives
I can find the missing number to balance a calculation.

To solve the jokes, work out the answer and write it in the circle. Then use the grid to find the letter that goes with each answer and write it on the line. The first one is done for you!

27	10	18	5	30	40	50	6	15	8
A	M	K	T	O	H	N	E	Y	S

What doesn't get wet when it rains?

T _ _ _ / _ _ _ _ !

$20 + (5) = 100 \div 4$

$3 \times 11 = \bigcirc - 7$

$30 \times 4 = \bigcirc \times 20$

$3 \times \bigcirc = 240 \div 10$

$4 \times \bigcirc = 40 - 16$

$\bigcirc + 22 = 7 \times 7$

What kind of key can't open any doors?

_ / _ _ _ _ -

_ _ _ _ !

$62 - 53 = \bigcirc \div 3$

$64 \div 4 = 160 \div \bigcirc$

$500 \div 10 = 20 + \bigcirc$

$\bigcirc + 15 = 13 \times 5$

$\bigcirc \times 2 = 30 + 6$

$30 + \bigcirc = 6 \times 6$

$5 \times 6 = \bigcirc \times 2$

Year 5 – Multiplication and division
* Solve problems involving addition, subtraction, multiplication and division and a combination of these, including understanding the meaning of the equals sign.

Compare and order fractions (1)

Learning objectives
I can compare fractions where the denominators are multiples of the same number.

To solve the jokes, work out which is the largest fraction. Write the answer in the circle, then use the grid to find the letter that goes with each answer and write it on the line. The first one is done for you.

5/6	3/3	4/5	7/9	8/12	3/8	7/8	5/8	7/14	6/10	8/9	1/4	4/10
P	N	E	C	A	H	S	I	B	K	L	O	T

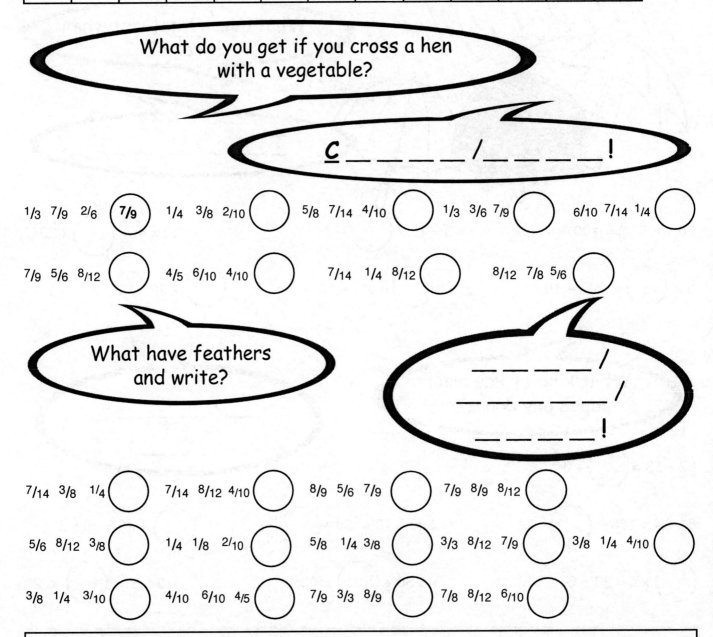

What do you get if you cross a hen with a vegetable?

C _ _ _ _ _ / _ _ _ _ _ !

What have feathers and write?

_ _ _ _ _ /
_ _ _ _ _ /
_ _ _ _ _ !

Year 5 – Fractions (including decimals and percentages)
* *Compare and order fractions whose denominators are all multiples of the same number.*

Compare and order fractions (2)

Learning objectives
I can compare fractions where the denominators are multiples of the same number.

To solve the jokes, work out which is the largest fraction. Write the answer in the circle, then use the grid to find the letter that goes with each answer and write it on the line. The first one is done for you!

3/12	2/5	5/6	2/2	4/5	7/9	8/12	4/8	2/6	5/8
T	W	K	D	E	Q	R	L	U	S

1/16	7/14	6/9	6/10	1/12
M	A	P	C	I

What do ducks pull at Christmas?

Q_ _ _ _ _ - _ _ _ _ !

1/3 7/9 2/6 (7/9)   1/9 3/12 2/6 ( )   1/16 7/14 3/12 ( )   6/10 2/5 4/10 ( )   1/9 5/6 3/12 ( )

4/5 6/10 2/5 ( )   8/12 1/16 4/8 ( )   6/10 3/12 5/8 ( )

What do you call a vampire duck?

_ _ _ _ - _ _ _ !

4/8 2/2 8/12 ( )   2/6 1/9 1/12 ( )   2/5 6/10 3/10 ( )   5/6 1/12 1/9 ( )

1/16 2/6 3/12 ( )   4/8 1/12 1/16 ( )   2/6 3/12 7/14 ( )

Year 5 – Fractions (including decimals and percentages)
- *Compare and order fractions whose denominators are all multiples of the same number.*

Improper fractions and mixed numbers (1)

Learning objectives
I can convert an improper fraction to a mixed number and vice versa.

122 25%
÷ 3/12 =
XVII 0.25

To solve the jokes, write the answer in the circle. Then use the grid to find the letter that goes with each answer and write it on the line. The first one is done for you.

$3/2$	$7/4$	$1\frac{1}{2}$	$5/3$	$2\frac{1}{4}$	$7/5$	$1\frac{2}{5}$	$9/5$	$3\frac{2}{3}$	$2\frac{3}{5}$	$3\frac{1}{2}$
O	D	C	T	W	H	S	E	F	A	R

What is a bird's favourite part of the news?

I _ _ _ /
_ _ _ _ _ _ _ _ /
_ _ _ _ _ _ _ _ _ !

$1\frac{2}{3}$ (⑤/₃) $1\frac{2}{5}$ ◯ $1\frac{4}{5}$ ◯

$11/3$ ◯ $1\frac{4}{5}$ ◯ $13/5$ ◯ $1\frac{2}{3}$ ◯ $1\frac{2}{5}$ ◯ $1\frac{4}{5}$ ◯ $7/2$ ◯

$11/3$ ◯ $1\frac{1}{2}$ ◯ $7/2$ ◯ $1\frac{4}{5}$ ◯ $3/2$ ◯ $13/5$ ◯ $7/5$ ◯ $1\frac{2}{3}$ ◯

What do you get if you cross a lawnmower with a budgie?

_ _ _ _ _ _ _ _ _ _ / _ _ _ _ _ !

$7/5$ ◯ $1\frac{2}{5}$ ◯ $7/2$ ◯ $1\frac{4}{5}$ ◯ $1\frac{3}{4}$ ◯ $1\frac{3}{4}$ ◯ $1\frac{4}{5}$ ◯ $1\frac{3}{4}$ ◯

$1\frac{2}{3}$ ◯ $9/4$ ◯ $1\frac{4}{5}$ ◯ $1\frac{4}{5}$ ◯ $1\frac{2}{3}$ ◯

Year 5 – Fractions (including decimals and percentages)
- *Recognise mixed numbers and improper fractions and convert from one form to the other and write mathematical statements > 1 as a mixed number for example, $\frac{2}{5} + \frac{4}{5} = \frac{6}{5} = 1\frac{1}{5}$.*

Improper fractions and mixed numbers (2)

Learning objectives
I can convert an improper fraction to a mixed number and vice versa.

25%
$\div$ $3/12$ =
XVII 0.25

To solve the jokes, write the answer in the circle. Then use the grid to find the letter that goes with each answer and write it on the line. The first one is done for you.

$2\frac{5}{8}$	$9/2$	$1\frac{1}{7}$	$11/4$	$3\frac{1}{2}$	$14/3$	$16/7$	$3\frac{3}{4}$	$20/9$	$17/5$	$5\frac{3}{5}$	$22/5$	$3\frac{1}{3}$	$2\frac{4}{5}$	$19/4$	$7\frac{1}{2}$
I	T	P	U	H	L	R	E	S	C	A	D	N	O	G	B

What takes injured insects to hospital?

T _ _ _ /

_ _ _ _ - _ _ _ _ _ _ _ _ !

$4\frac{1}{2}$ (9/2) $7/2$ ◯ $15/4$ ◯

$28/5$ ◯ $10/3$ ◯ $4\frac{1}{2}$ ◯

$15/2$ ◯ $2\frac{3}{4}$ ◯ $4\frac{2}{3}$ ◯ $28/5$ ◯ $10/3$ ◯ $3\frac{2}{5}$ ◯ $15/4$ ◯

What are caterpillars afraid of?

_ _ _ _ _ _ _ / _ _ _ _ _ _ _ _ !

$4\frac{2}{5}$ ◯ $14/5$ ◯ $4\frac{3}{4}$ ◯ $4\frac{3}{4}$ ◯ $15/4$ ◯ $2\frac{2}{7}$ ◯

$8/7$ ◯ $21/8$ ◯ $4\frac{2}{3}$ ◯ $4\frac{2}{3}$ ◯ $28/5$ ◯ $2\frac{2}{7}$ ◯ $2\frac{2}{9}$ ◯

Year 5 – Fractions (including decimals and percentages)
- *Recognise mixed numbers and improper fractions and convert from one form to the other and write mathematical statements > 1 as a mixed number for example, $\frac{2}{5} + \frac{4}{5} = \frac{6}{5} = 1\frac{1}{5}$.*

Adding and subtracting fractions (1)

Learning objectives
I can add and subtract fractions with the same denominator.
I can add and subtract fractions with denominators that are multiples of the same number.
If the answer is an improper fraction, I can turn it into a mixed number

To solve the joke, work out the answer to the fractions question. Write the answer in the circle, then use the grid to find the letter that goes with each answer and write it on the line. The first one is done for you!

$1\frac{2}{5}$	$\frac{5}{8}$	$\frac{7}{9}$	$1\frac{4}{9}$	$\frac{3}{4}$	$2\frac{5}{6}$	$\frac{2}{5}$	$\frac{7}{8}$	$\frac{7}{10}$	$2\frac{4}{10}$
F	O	R	N	S	I	E	U	W	P

$\frac{3}{8}$	$\frac{6}{7}$	$3\frac{3}{5}$	$1\frac{1}{7}$
A	T	L	H

> Where did the spider go when he got angry?

U _ _ / _ _ _ _ / _ _ _ _ _ !

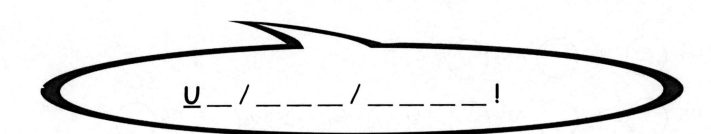

$\frac{10}{4} - \frac{13}{8} = \left(\frac{7}{8}\right)$ $\frac{8}{10} + \frac{16}{10} = \bigcirc$

$\frac{21}{7} - \frac{30}{14} = \bigcirc$ $\frac{5}{7} + \frac{6}{14} = \bigcirc$ $\frac{13}{5} - \frac{22}{10} = \bigcirc$

$\frac{13}{5} - \frac{19}{10} = \bigcirc$ $\frac{15}{8} - \frac{6}{4} = \bigcirc$ $\frac{10}{5} + \frac{8}{5} = \bigcirc$ $\frac{22}{5} - \frac{4}{5} = \bigcirc$

Year 5 – Fractions (including decimals and percentages)
- *Add and subtract fractions with the same denominator and denominators that are multiples of the same number*
- *recognise mixed numbers and improper fractions and convert from one form to the other and write mathematical statements > 1 as a mixed number for example, $\frac{2}{5} + \frac{4}{5} = \frac{6}{5} = 1\frac{1}{5}$.*

Adding and subtracting fractions (2)

Learning objectives
I can add and subtract fractions with the same denominator.
I can add and subtract fractions with denominators that are multiples
   of the same number.
If the answer is an improper fraction, I can turn it into a mixed number

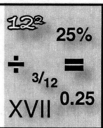

*To solve the joke, work out the answer to the fractions question. Write the answer in the circle,
then use the grid to find the letter that goes with each answer and write it on the line. The first one
is done for you!*

$1\frac{2}{5}$	$\frac{5}{8}$	$\frac{7}{9}$	$1\frac{4}{9}$	$\frac{3}{4}$	$2\frac{5}{6}$	$\frac{2}{5}$	$\frac{7}{8}$	$\frac{7}{10}$	$2\frac{4}{10}$
F	O	R	N	S	I	E	U	W	P

$\frac{3}{8}$	$\frac{6}{7}$	$3\frac{3}{5}$	$1\frac{1}{7}$
A	T	L	H

> Why did the spider go out in his car?

> F _ _ / _ / _ _ _ _ !

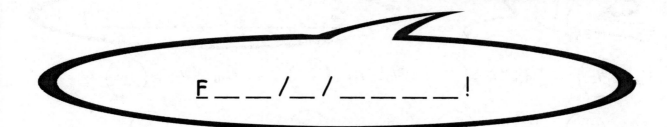

$\frac{16}{5} - \frac{9}{5} =$ ($1\frac{2}{5}$)

$\frac{8}{4} - \frac{11}{8} =$ ◯

$\frac{19}{9} - \frac{4}{3} =$ ◯

$\frac{26}{8} - \frac{23}{8} =$ ◯

$\frac{24}{8} - \frac{9}{4} =$ ◯

$\frac{13}{10} + \frac{11}{10} =$ ◯

$\frac{23}{6} - \frac{6}{6} =$ ◯

$\frac{8}{9} + \frac{5}{9} =$ ◯

Year 5 – Fractions (including decimals and percentages)
- *Add and subtract fractions with the same denominator and denominators that are multiples of the same number*
- *recognise mixed numbers and improper fractions and convert from one form to the other and write mathematical statements > 1 as a mixed number for example, $\frac{2}{5} + \frac{4}{5} = \frac{6}{5} = 1\frac{1}{5}$.*

Adding and subtracting fractions (3)

Learning objectives
I can add and subtract fractions with the same denominator.
I can add and subtract fractions with denominators that are multiples of the same number.
If the answer is an improper fraction, I can turn it into a mixed number.

122 25%
÷ $3/12$ =
XVII 0.25

To solve the jokes, work out the answer to the fractions question. Write the answer in the circle, then use the grid to find the letter that goes with each answer and write it on the line. The first one is done for you!

$1\,^5/_8$	$^2/_3$	$^5/_8$	$^3/_4$	$3\,^1/_5$	$2\,^2/_3$	$^3/_5$	$^4/_5$	$^6/_7$	$2\,^7/_{10}$
P	G	A	E	I	R	P	O	H	Y

What do old rabbits have?

$\underline{G}$ _ _ _ _ / _ _ _ _ !

$^2/_6 + ^3/_9 =$ ⟨$^2/_3$⟩ $\qquad$ $^8/_6 + ^{12}/_9 =$ ◯ $\qquad$ $^{12}/_8 - ^9/_{12} =$ ◯ $\qquad$ $^{12}/_{10} + ^{15}/_{10} =$ ◯

$^{10}/_7 - ^8/_{14} =$ ◯ $\qquad$ $^7/_4 - ^9/_8 =$ ◯ $\qquad$ $^{12}/_3 - ^8/_6 =$ ◯ $\qquad$ $^1/_2 + ^1/_4 =$ ◯

What is a rabbit's favourite type of music?

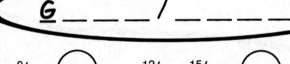

_ _ _ _ / _ _ _ _ !

$^{10}/_{14} + ^3/_{21} =$ ◯ $\qquad$ $^{10}/_5 + ^6/_5 =$ ◯ $\qquad$ $^{10}/_5 - ^{14}/_{10} =$ ◯

$21/_7 - ^{15}/_7 =$ ◯ $\qquad$ $^4/_{10} + ^2/_5 =$ ◯ $\qquad$ $^8/_5 - ^{10}/_{10} =$ ◯

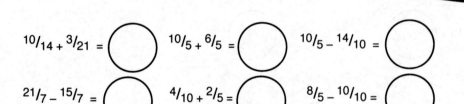

Year 5 – Fractions (including decimals and percentages)
- *Add and subtract fractions with the same denominator and denominators that are multiples of the same number*
- *recognise mixed numbers and improper fractions and convert from one form to the other and write mathematical statements > 1 as a mixed number for example, $^2/_5 + ^4/_5 = ^6/_5 = 1\,^1/_5$.*

Multiplying fractions (1)

Learning objectives
I can multiply a proper fraction or a mixed number by a whole number.

12^2 25%
$\div$ $3/12$ =
XVII 0.25

To solve the jokes, work out the answer to the fractions question. Write the answer in the circle, then use the grid to find the letter that goes with each answer and write it on the line. The first one is done for you!

$2\frac{1}{3}$	$\frac{8}{9}$	3	$2\frac{1}{2}$	$4\frac{1}{2}$	$1\frac{1}{5}$	$3\frac{1}{5}$	$2\frac{2}{3}$	$4\frac{4}{5}$	$\frac{6}{7}$
S	F	A	O	D	M	E	L	R	B

What are white, furry and live in your mouth?

M _ _ _ _ _ / _ _ _ _ _ _ !

$\frac{2}{5} \times 3 = \left(1\frac{1}{5}\right)$ $\frac{1}{2} \times 5 = \bigcirc$ $\frac{2}{3} \times 4 = \bigcirc$ $\frac{3}{4} \times 4 = \bigcirc$ $2\frac{2}{5} \times 2 = \bigcirc$

$\frac{2}{7} \times 3 = \bigcirc$ $\frac{4}{5} \times 4 = \bigcirc$ $1\frac{2}{4} \times 2 = \bigcirc$ $1\frac{3}{5} \times 3 = \bigcirc$ $\frac{1}{3} \times 7 = \bigcirc$

What do you call a bald teddy?

_ _ _ _ _ /
_ _ _ _ _ !

$\frac{2}{9} \times 4 = \bigcirc$ $1\frac{1}{5} \times 4 = \bigcirc$ $1\frac{3}{5} \times 2 = \bigcirc$ $1\frac{1}{2} \times 3 = \bigcirc$

$\frac{2}{7} \times 3 = \bigcirc$ $\frac{4}{5} \times 4 = \bigcirc$ $\frac{3}{6} \times 6 = \bigcirc$ $\frac{4}{5} \times 6 = \bigcirc$

Year 5 – Fractions (including decimals and percentages)
• *Multiply proper fractions and mixed numbers by whole numbers, supported by materials and diagrams*

Learning objectives
I can multiply a proper fraction or a mixed number by a whole number.

122 25%
÷ 3/12 =
XVII 0.25

To solve the jokes, work out the answer to the fractions question. Write the answer in the circle, then use the grid to find the letter that goes with each answer and write it on the line. The first one is done for you!

$3\tfrac{3}{7}$	$\tfrac{9}{10}$	5	$4\tfrac{1}{2}$	$4\tfrac{1}{4}$	$\tfrac{6}{7}$	$3\tfrac{1}{5}$	$4\tfrac{2}{3}$	$3\tfrac{1}{3}$
F	A	U	W	S	E	T	R	O

What do you get if you cross a dog with a monster?

<u>A</u> / _ _ _ _ _ - _ _ _ _ _ !

$\tfrac{3}{10} \times 3 = \left(\tfrac{9}{10}\right)$ $1\tfrac{1}{2} \times 3 = \bigcirc$ $\tfrac{1}{7} \times 6 = \bigcirc$ $\tfrac{2}{3} \times 7 = \bigcirc$ $\tfrac{2}{7} \times 3 = \bigcirc$

$\tfrac{1}{2} \times 9 = \bigcirc$ $\tfrac{2}{3} \times 5 = \bigcirc$ $1\tfrac{2}{3} \times 2 = \bigcirc$ $\tfrac{3}{7} \times 8 = \bigcirc$

What did the dog say when it sat on sandpaper?

_ _ _ _ _ !

$2\tfrac{1}{3} \times 2 = \bigcirc$ $2\tfrac{1}{2} \times 2 = \bigcirc$ $1\tfrac{1}{7} \times 3 = \bigcirc$ $1\tfrac{5}{7} \times 2 = \bigcirc$

Year 5 – Fractions (including decimals and percentages)
- *Multiply proper fractions and mixed numbers by whole numbers, supported by materials and diagrams*

Rounding decimals (1)

Learning objectives
I can round a decimal number to the nearest whole number or to one decimal place.

12² 25%
÷ 3/12 =
XVII 0.25

To solve the first joke, round each number to the nearest whole number and write the answer in the circle. Then use the grid to find the letter that goes with each answer and write it on the line. The first one has been done for you!

1	3	7	5	2	4	8	6
F	S	E	L	R	A	Y	T

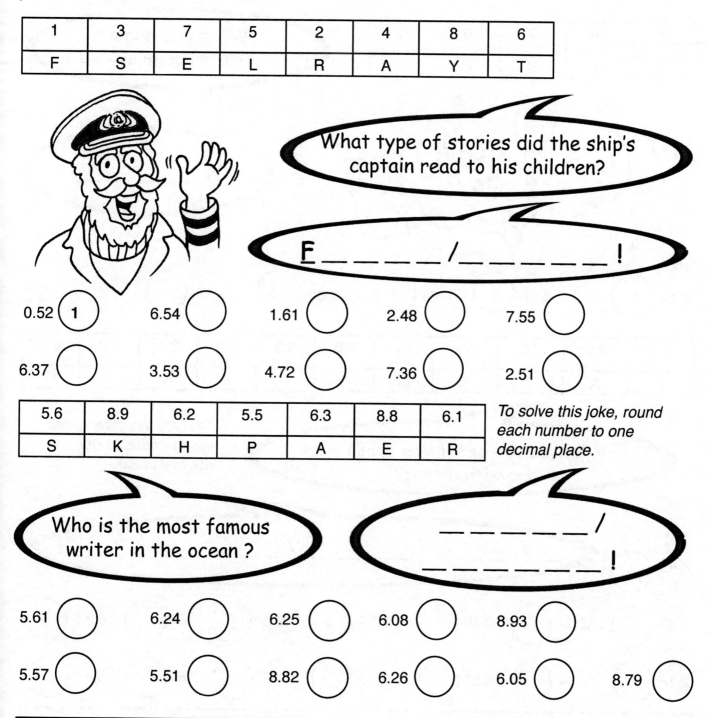

What type of stories did the ship's captain read to his children?

F _ _ _ _ _ _ _ / _ _ _ _ _ _ _ !

0.52 (1)   6.54 ( )   1.61 ( )   2.48 ( )   7.55 ( )

6.37 ( )   3.53 ( )   4.72 ( )   7.36 ( )   2.51 ( )

5.6	8.9	6.2	5.5	6.3	8.8	6.1
S	K	H	P	A	E	R

To solve this joke, round each number to one decimal place.

Who is the most famous writer in the ocean ?

_ _ _ _ _ _ _ /
_ _ _ _ _ _ _ !

5.61 ( )   6.24 ( )   6.25 ( )   6.08 ( )   8.93 ( )

5.57 ( )   5.51 ( )   8.82 ( )   6.26 ( )   6.05 ( )   8.79 ( )

Year 5 – Fractions (including decimals and percenytages)
* *Round decimals with two decimal places to the nearest whole number and to one decimal place.*

Rounding decimals (2)

Learning objectives
I can round a decimal number to the nearest whole number or to one decimal place.

To solve the first joke, round each number to the nearest whole number and write the answer in the circle. Then use the grid to find the letter that goes with each answer and write it on the line. The first one has been done for you!

9	10	7	6	8
W	N	H	E	I

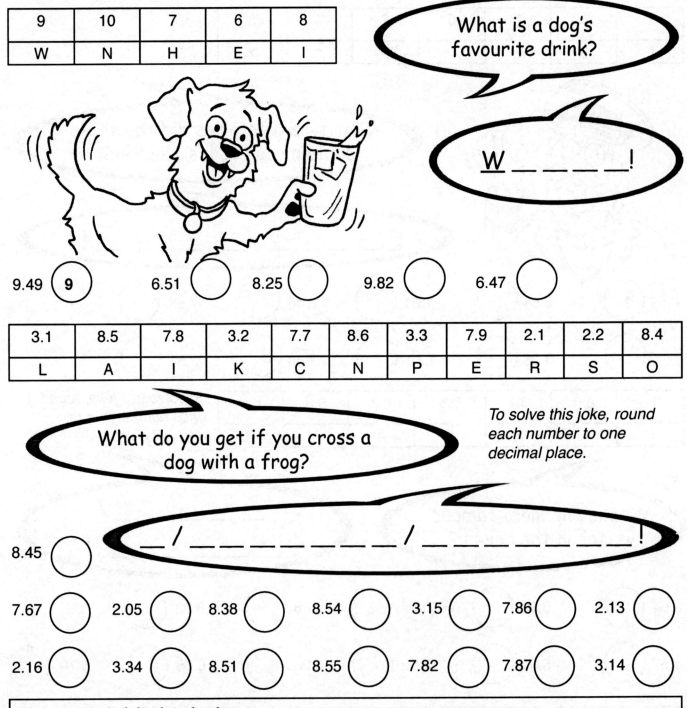

What is a dog's favourite drink?

W _ _ _ _ _ _ !

9.49 (9)   6.51 ( )   8.25 ( )   9.82 ( )   6.47 ( )

3.1	8.5	7.8	3.2	7.7	8.6	3.3	7.9	2.1	2.2	8.4
L	A	I	K	C	N	P	E	R	S	O

What do you get if you cross a dog with a frog?

To solve this joke, round each number to one decimal place.

_ _ / _ _ _ _ _ _ _ _ / _ _ _ _ _ _ !

8.45 ( )

7.67 ( )   2.05 ( )   8.38 ( )   8.54 ( )   3.15 ( )   7.86 ( )   2.13 ( )

2.16 ( )   3.34 ( )   8.51 ( )   8.55 ( )   7.82 ( )   7.87 ( )   3.14 ( )

Year 5 – Fractions (including decimals and percentages
• *Round decimals with two decimal places to the nearest whole number and to one decimal place.*

Comparing decimals up to 3 places (1)

Learning objectives
I can show that I understand the place value of decimals by finding the largest one.

To solve the joke, work out which is the largest decimal number in each group and write it in the circle. Then use the grid to find the letter that goes with each answer and write it on the line. The first one is done for you!

2.3	4.099	3.15	4.09	2.55	3.055	4.191	3.1	2.23	5.3	4.109
T	R	P	F	U	D	I	M	E	N	S

What do dogs have that no other animal has?

3.15	2.5	3.055	
3.102	2.055	3.1	
3.12 **(3.15)**	2.55 ◯	3.15 ◯	
3.055	2.23	3.113	

P _ _ _ _ _ _ !

2.9	4.099	2.23	4.101
3.15	4.109	2.203	4.1
3.09 ◯	4.191 ◯	2.032 ◯	4.099 ◯
3.015	4.09	2.2	4.109

Year 5 – Fractions (including decimals and percentages)
* *Read, write, order and compare numbers with up to three decimal places.*

Comparing decimals up to 3 places (2)

Learning objectives
I can show that I understand the place value of decimals by finding the largest one.

To solve the joke, work out which is the largest decimal number in each group and write it in the oval. Then use the grid to find the letter that goes with each answer and write it on the line. The first one is done for you!

2.3	4.099	3.15	4.09	2.55	3.055	4.191	3.1	2.23	5.3	4.109
T	R	P	F	U	D	I	M	E	N	S

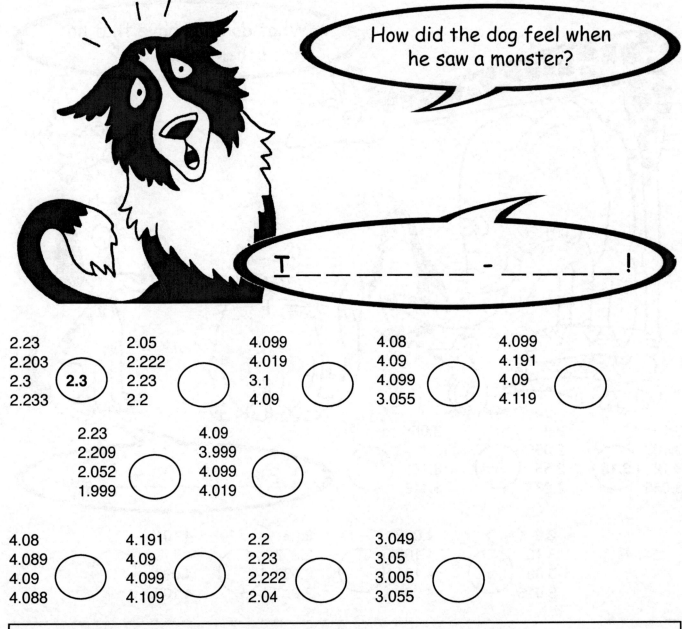

How did the dog feel when he saw a monster?

T _ _ _ _ _ _ - _ _ _ _ !

2.23
2.203
2.3   (2.3)
2.233

2.05
2.222
2.23
2.2

4.099
4.019
3.1
4.09

4.08
4.09
4.099
3.055

4.099
4.191
4.09
4.119

2.23
2.209
2.052
1.999

4.09
3.999
4.099
4.019

4.08
4.089
4.09
4.088

4.191
4.09
4.099
4.109

2.2
2.23
2.222
2.04

3.049
3.05
3.005
3.055

Year 5 – Fractions (including decimals and percentages)
• *Read, write, order and compare numbers with up to three decimal places.*

Comparing decimals up to 3 places (3)

Learning objectives
I can show that I understand the place value of decimals by finding the largest one.

12² 25%
÷ ³/₁₂ =
XVII 0.25

To solve the joke, work out which is the largest decimal number in each group and write it in the oval. Then use the grid to find the letter that goes with each answer and write it on the line. The first one is done for you!

5.2	6.65	7.54	5.102	6.6	7.445	5.012	7.455	6.56	5.12	7.5	6.556	7.454
S	B	D	H	R	O	G	I	L	C	T	E	U

What is a penguin's favourite part of a salad?

I _ _ _ _ _ _ _ /
_ _ _ _ _ _ _ !

7.454	5.12	6.065	6.56	6.556	6.56	5.009
7.445	5.102	6.06	6.6	6.55	6.6	5.010
7.455	5.012	6.55	6.65	6.065	6.556	5.012
7.45	5.1	6.556	6.556	5.2	6.50	5.011

(7.455) ◯ ◯ ◯ ◯ ◯ ◯

6.56	6.556	7.445	7.454	7.445	5.012	6.5
6.065	6.506	7.5	7.445	7.454	5.102	6.556
6.55	6.5	7.454	7.455	7.4	5.12	6.506
6.505	6.066	7.455	7.5	7.405	5.112	6.55

◯ ◯ ◯ ◯ ◯ ◯ ◯

Year 5 – Fractions (including decimals and percentages)
• *Read, write, order and compare numbers with up to three decimal places.*

Comparing decimals up to 3 places (4)

Learning objectives
I can show that I understand the place value of decimals by finding the largest one.

122 25%
÷ 3/12 =
XVII 0.25

To solve the joke, work out which is the largest decimal number in each group and write it in the ovals. Then use the grid to find the letter that goes with each answer and write it on the line. The first one is done for you!

5.2	6.65	7.54	5.102	6.6	7.445	5.012	7.455	6.56	5.12	7.5	6.556	7.454
S	B	D	H	R	O	G	I	L	C	T	E	U

Which side of a penguin has the most feathers?

O _ _ - _ _ _ _ !

7.445	7.4	7.454	5.12	7.4	7.455	5.666
7.4	7.454	7.5	5.2	7.445	7.454	6.066
7.405	7.445	7.445	5.012	7.455	7.54	6.506
7.154	4.755	7.455	5.102	7.454	7.5	6.556

(7.445) ( ) ( ) ( ) ( ) ( ) ( )

Year 5 – Fractions (including decimals and percentages)
• *Read, write, order and compare numbers with up to three decimal places.*

Fraction, decimal and percentage equivalents (1)

Learning objectives
I can write equivalent fractions, decimals and percentages.

To solve the joke, find the equivalent fraction, decimal or percentage and write the answer in the circle. Then use the grid to find the letter that goes with each answer and write it on the line. The first one is done for you!

1/2	2/5	57/100	1/4	80%	50%	0.3	0.4	25%	45/100
K	H	E	I	U	S	P	A	F	N

1/5	20%	0.8	0.25
O	D	R	M

What do snakes do after they fall out?

H _ _ _ _ / _ _ _ _ / _ _ _ _ / _ _ !

0.4 as a fraction **(2/5)**

25% as a fraction ( )

20/40 as a percentage ( )

0.5 as a percentage ( )

2/5 as a decimal ( )

45% as a fraction ( )

1/5 as a percentage ( )

1/4 as a decimal ( )

40% as a decimal ( )

25/50 as a fraction ( )

57% as a fraction ( )

0.8 as a percentage ( )

6/20 as a decimal ( )

Year 5 – Fractions (including decimals and percentages)
- *Recognise the percent symbol (%) and understand that per cent relates to 'number of parts per hundred', and write percentages as a fraction with denominator 100, and as a decimal.*
- *Solve problems which require knowing percentage and decimal equivalents of $1/2$, $1/4$, $1/5$, $2/5$, $4/5$ and those fractions with a denominator of a multiple of 10 or 25.*

Fraction, decimal and percentage equivalents (2)

Learning objectives
I can write equivalent fractions, decimals and percentages.

123 25%
÷ 3/12 =
XVII 0.25

To solve the joke, find the equivalent fraction, decimal or percentage and write the answer in the oval. Then use the grid to find the letter that goes with each answer and write it on the line.

¹/₂	²/₅	⁵⁷/₁₀₀	¹/₄	80%	50%	0.3	0.4	25%	⁴⁵/₁₀₀
K	H	E	I	U	S	P	A	F	N

¹/₅	20%	0.8	0.25
O	D	R	M

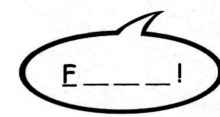

How many words are in 'The Oxford English Dictionary'?

F _ _ _ _ !

0.25 as a percentage	0.2 as a fraction	⁸/₁₀ as a percentage	⁴/₅ as a decimal
(25%)	( )	( )	( )

Year 5 – Fractions (including decimals and percentages)
* *Recognise the percent symbol (%) and understand that per cent relates to 'number of parts per hundred', and write percentages as a fraction with denominator 100, and as a decimal.*
* *Solve problems which require knowing percentage and decimal equivalents of* ¹/₂ *,* ¹/₄ *,* ¹/₅ *,* ²/₅ *,* ⁴/₅ *and those fractions with a denominator of a multiple of 10 or 25.*

Fraction, decimal and percentage equivalents (3)

Learning objectives
I can write equivalent fractions, decimals and percentages.

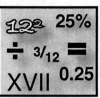

To solve the joke, find the equivalent fraction, decimal or percentage and write the answer in the oval. Then use the grid to find the letter that goes with each answer and write it on the line. The first one is done for you!

4/5	2/5	65/100	60%	0.4	25%	80%	0.2
H	I	C	T	G	S	L	E

What happened to the cold jellyfish?

I̲ _ _ / _ _ _ _ _ !

0.4 as a fraction (2/5)

3/5 as a percentage ( )

1/4 as a percentage ( )

1/5 as a decimal ( )

0.6 as a percentage ( )

What note did the pirate sing?

_ _ _ _ _ / _ _ !

80% as a fraction ( )

40% as a fraction ( )

2/5 as a decimal ( )

0.8 as a fraction ( )

0.65 as a fraction ( )

Place value and ordering (1)

To solve the joke, use place value to work out the value of the underlined digit. Then use the grid to find the letter that goes with each answer and write it on the line. The first one is done for you!

9,000,000	500	600,000	3,000,000	90,000	50,000	6,000,000	300,000
L	P	A	Y	T	S	N	H

900,000	3,000
M	E

> What do you call an elephant that doesn't wash?
>
> S̲ _ _ _ _ _ _ - _ _ _ _ _ _ !

6**5**2,135
(50,000)

1,**9**31,111
( )

24**3**,380
( )

9,121,131
( )

9,147,111
( )

3,258,159
( )

9,436,**5**78
( )

3,**3**52,198
( )

2,**6**58,497
( )

6,258,166
( )

9,6**9**4,535
( )

Year 6 – Number and place value
- *Read, write, order and compare numbers up to 10,000,000 and determine the value of each digit.*

Place value and ordering (2)

Learning objectives
I know the value of each digit in numbers up to 10,000,000.
I can use place value to say which is the largest number.

122 25%
÷ 3/12 =
XVII 0.25

To solve the joke, use place value to work out which is the largest number. Then use the grid to find the letter that goes with each answer and write it on the line. The first one is done for you!

2,865,039	4,125,608	1,865,093	2,354,354	4,125,806	4,124,086	2,354,543	2,865,309
K	R	S	N	U	D	T	A

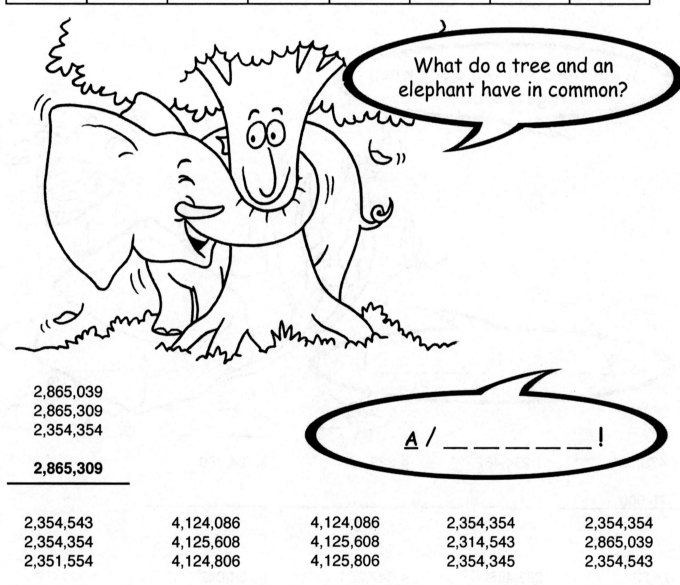

What do a tree and an elephant have in common?

2,865,039
2,865,309
2,354,354

2,865,309
_____

A / _ _ _ _ _ _ !

2,354,543	4,124,086	4,124,086	2,354,354	2,354,354
2,354,354	4,125,608	4,125,608	2,314,543	2,865,039
2,351,554	4,124,806	4,125,806	2,354,345	2,354,543

_____ _____ _____ _____ _____

Year 6 – Number and place value
- *Read, write, order and compare numbers up to 10,000,000 and determine the value of each digit.*

Place value and ordering (3)

Learning objectives
I know the value of each digit in numbers up to 10,000,000.

1 2 3   25%
÷ 3/12 =
XVII   0.25

To solve the joke, use place value to work out the value of the underlined digit. Then use the grid to find the letter that goes with each answer and write it on the line. The first one is done for you!

70,000	40,000	200,000	700,000	800,000	4,000,000	20,000	8,000,000
K	R	E	S	N	L	M	P

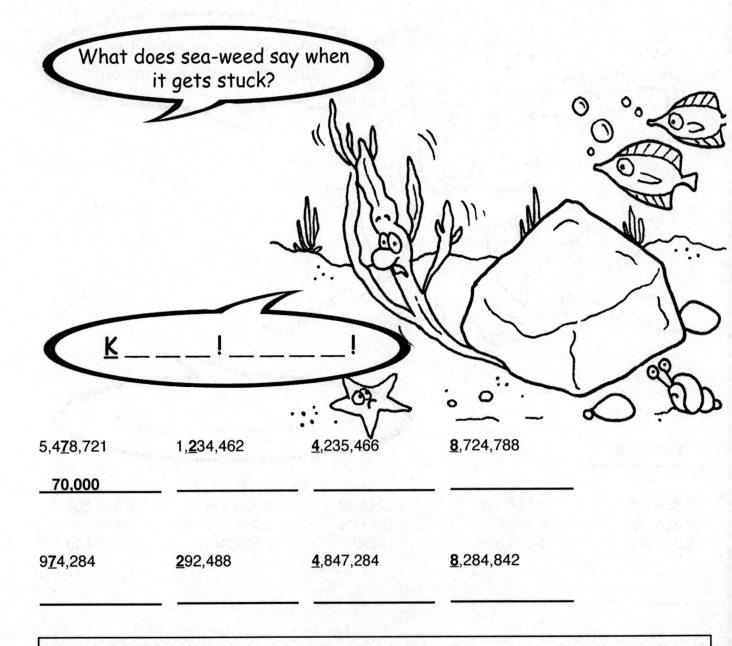

What does sea-weed say when it gets stuck?

<u>K</u> _ _ _ ! _ _ _ _ !

5,4<u>7</u>8,721   1,<u>2</u>34,462   <u>4</u>,235,466   <u>8</u>,724,788

<u>70,000</u>   _____   _____   _____

9<u>7</u>4,284   <u>2</u>92,488   <u>4</u>,847,284   <u>8</u>,284,842

_____   _____   _____   _____

Year 6 – Number and place value
• *Read, write, order and compare numbers up to 10,000,000 and determine the value of each digit.*

Place value and ordering (4)

Learning objectives
I know the value of each digit in numbers up to 10,000,000.
I can use place value to say which is the largest number.

123 25%
÷ 3/12 =
XVII 0.25

To solve the joke, use place value to work out which is the largest number. Then use the grid to find the letter that goes with each answer and write it on the line. The first one is done for you!

3,465,587	3,258,852	3,198,989	3,258,258	3,465,578	3,258,528	3,456,889	3,199,981
D	N	T	R	E	S	Y	O

What kind of stones will you never find in the sea?

D __ __ / __ __ __ __ __ !

3,465,578   3,258,258   3,258,258
3,456,889   3,198,989   3,456,889
3,465,587   3,199,981   3,456,789

3,465,587
_____   _____   _____

3,199,981   3,258,528   3,465,577   3,198,989
3,198,989   3,258,258   3,465,578   3,258,258
3,198,999   3,258,852   3,456,889   3,258,528

_____   _____   _____   _____

Year 6 – Number and place value
*   *Read, write, order and compare numbers up to 10,000,000 and determine the value of each digit.*

Negative numbers (1)

Learning objectives
I can find the difference between two temperatures, including negative numbers.

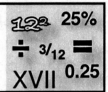

To solve the joke, find the difference between the temperatures on the scales and write the answer in the circle. Then use the grid to find the letter that goes with each answer and write it on the line. The first one is done for you!

14	7	15	6	20	2	0	5	3	8	10
S	C	O	T	A	I	B	F	E	R	N

Year 6 – Number and place value
- *Use negative numbers in context, and calculate intervals across zero.*

Negative numbers (2)

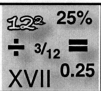

To solve the joke, find the difference between the temperatures on the scales and write the answer in the circle. Then use the grid to find the letter that goes with each answer and write it on the line. The first one is done for you!

14	7	15	6	20	2	0	5	3	8	10
S	C	O	T	A	I	B	F	E	R	N

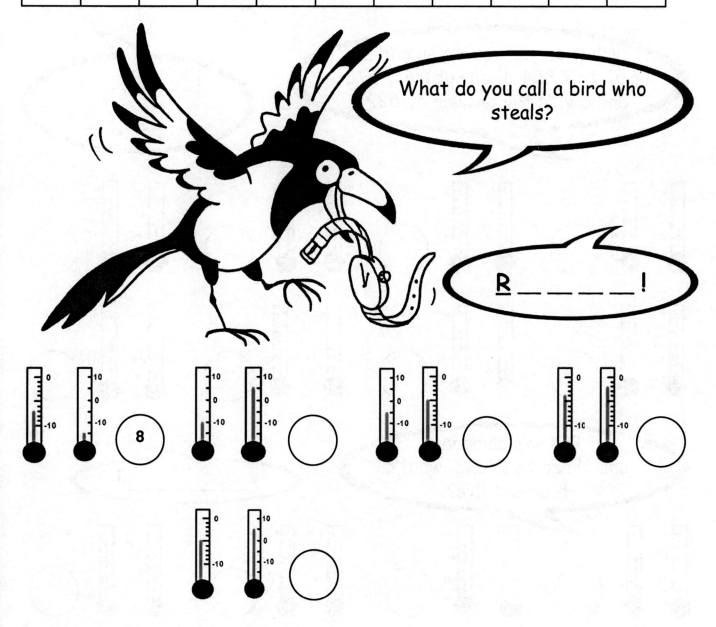

Negative numbers (3)

Learning objectives
I can find the difference between two temperatures, including negative numbers.

To solve the jokes, find the difference between the temperatures on the scales and write the answer in the circle. Then use the grid to find the letter that goes with each answer and write it on the line.

1	5	20	8	4	3	11	9	2	10
H	N	C	I	S	A	P	E	U	D

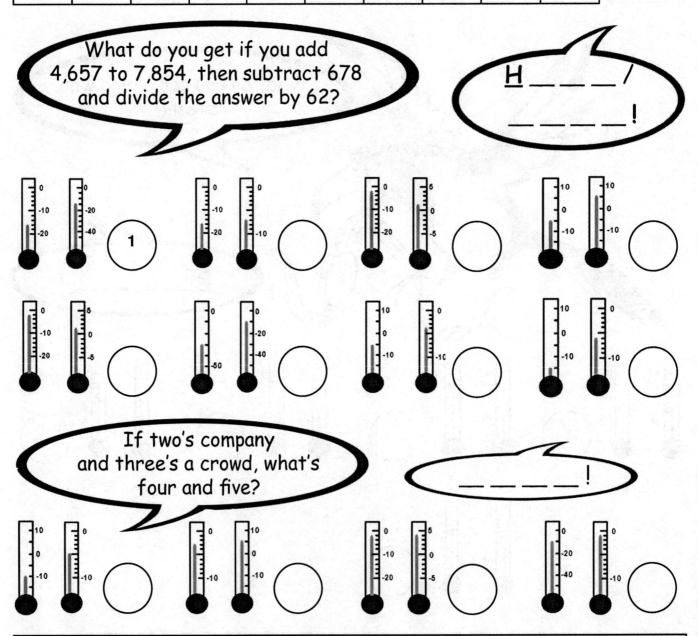

What do you get if you add 4,657 to 7,854, then subtract 678 and divide the answer by 62?

H _ _ _ _ /
_ _ _ _ _ !

If two's company and three's a crowd, what's four and five?

_ _ _ _ _ !

Long multiplication (1)

Learning objectives
I can use a written method to multiply numbers up to 4-digits by a 2-digit number.

122 25%
÷ 3/12 =
XVII 0.25

To solve the joke, do the calculation using the written method of long multiplication. Then use the grid to find the letter that goes with each answer and write it on the line. The first one has been done for you!

9150	88,524	41,262	155,652	40,968	115,720	56,126	19,305	35,258	32,120	67,648	25,026
H	S	I	E	A	R	O	F	L	P	T	U

4228 x 16
=
67,648

366 x 25
=

9156 x 17
=

2459 x 36
=

4009 x 14
=

258 x 97
=

4832 x 14
=

122 x 75
=

365 x 88
=

2954 x 19
=

1477 x 38
=

578 x 61
=

Year 6 – Addition, subtraction, multiplication and division
• *Multiply multi-digit numbers up to 4 digits by a two-digit whole number using the formal written method of long multiplication.*

Long multiplication (2)

Learning objectives
I can use a written method to multiply numbers up to 4-digits by a 2-digit number.

122 25%
÷ 3/12 =
XVII 0.25

To solve the joke, do the calculation using the written method of long multiplication. Then use the grid to find the letter that goes with each answer and write it in the speech bubble. The first one has been done for you!

9150	88,524	41,262	155,652	40,968	115,720	56,126	19,305	35,258	32,120	67,648	25,026
H	S	I	E	A	R	O	F	L	P	T	U

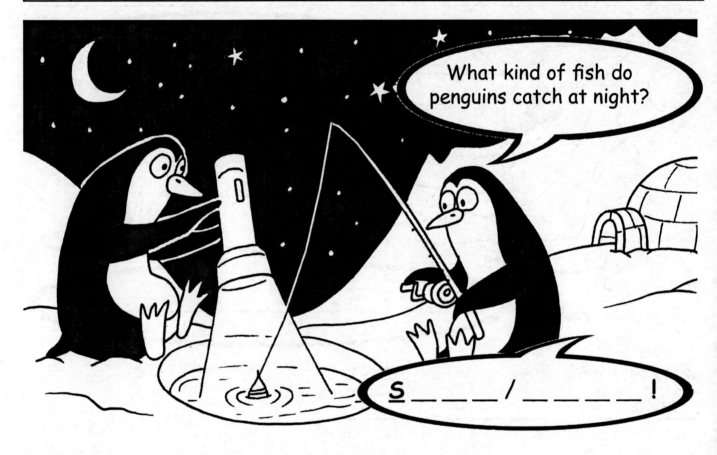

What kind of fish do penguins catch at night?

S ___ ___ ___ / ___ ___ ___ ___ !

4918 x 18 =   1208 x 56 =   569 x 72 =   1315 x 88 =

88,524   _____   _____   _____

495 x 39   897 x 46 =   7377 x 12 =   150 x 61 =

_____   _____   _____   _____

Year 6 – Addition, subtraction, multiplication and division
• *Multiply multi-digit numbers up to 4 digits by a two-digit whole number using the formal written method of long multiplication.*

Long multiplication (3)

Learning objectives
I can use a written method to multiply numbers up to 4-digits by a
2-digit number.

122 25%
÷ 3/12 =
XVII 0.25

To solve the joke, do the calculation using the written method of long multiplication. Then use the grid to find the letter that goes with each answer and write it in the speech bubble. The first one has been done for you!

76,084	9163	4288	10,620	612,105	84,640	6554	340,860	91,203
H	C	W	T	Y	A	M	K	O

62,888	58,536	4579	87,560	474,000	107,315
E	U	I	S	D	N

236 x 45 =

10,620
_____

3680 x 23 =

_____

3588 x 95 =

_____

4492 x 14 =

_____

2645 x 32 =

_____

268 x 16 =

_____

1840 x 46 =

_____

9417 x 65 =

_____

Year 6 – Addition, subtraction, multiplication and division
- *Multiply multi-digit numbers up to 4 digits by a two-digit whole number using the formal written method of long multiplication.*

Long multiplication (4)

To solve the joke, do the calculation using the written method of long multiplication. Then use the grid to find the letter that goes with each answer and write it in the speech bubble. The first one has been done for you!

76,084	9163	4288	10,620	612,105	84,640	6554	340,860	91,203
H	C	W	T	Y	A	M	K	O

62,888	58,536	4579	87,560	474,000	107,315
E	U	I	S	D	N

What are white on the outside, but grey and furry on the inside?

M _ _ _ _ _ / _ _ _ _ _ _ _ _ _ _ _ !

113 x 58
=
6554

2121 x 43
=

3252 x 18
=

1592 x 55
=

2246 x 28
=

1990 x 44
=

920 x 92
=

8255 x 13
=

9875 x 48
=

134 x 32
=

241 x 19
=

119 x 77
=

827 x 92
=

1123 x 56
=

995 x 88
=

Year 6 – Addition, subtraction, multiplication and division
* *Multiply multi-digit numbers up to 4 digits by a two-digit whole number using the formal written method of long multiplication.*

Long or short division (1)

Learning objectives
I can use a written method to divide numbers up to 4-digits by a
   2-digit number.

122 25%
÷ 3/12 =
XVII 0.25

To solve the joke, do the calculation using short or long division. Then use the grid to find the letter that goes with each answer and write it in the speech bubble. The first one has been done for you!

52	12	18	35	37	16	25	67	28
C	H	U	A	E	M	S	O	B

Where did the sheep
go on holiday?

B_ _ _ - _ _ _ _ _ _ !

$336 \div 12$
=
28
_____

$805 \div 23$
=
_____

$665 \div 19$
=
_____

$1140 \div 95$
=
_____

$735 \div 21$
=
_____

$1360 \div 85$
=
_____

$980 \div 28$
=
_____

$2450 \div 98$

_____

Year 6 – Addition, subtraction, multiplication and division
- *Divide numbers up to 4 digits by a two-digit whole number using the formal written method of long division, and interpret remainders as whole number remainders, fractions, or by rounding, as appropriate for the context*
- *Divide numbers up to 4 digits by a two-digit number using the formal written method of short division where appropriate, interpreting remainders according to the context.*

Long or short division (2)

Learning objectives
I can use a written method to divide numbers up to 4-digits by a 2-digit number.

122 25%
÷ 3/12 =
XVII 0.25

To solve the joke, do the calculation using short or long division. Then use the grid to find the letter that goes with each answer and write it in the speech bubble. The first one has been done for you!

52	12	18	35	37	16	25	67	28
C	H	U	A	E	M	S	O	B

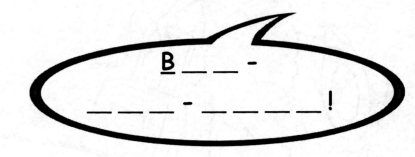

What do sheep cook on in the summer?

B _ _ -

_ _ _ - _ _ _ _ !

364 ÷ 13 =
28

840 ÷ 24 =

595 ÷ 17 =

532 ÷ 19 =

980 ÷ 28 =

455 ÷ 13 =

3952 ÷ 76 =

972 ÷ 54 =

2664 ÷ 72 =

1250 ÷ 50 =

Year 6 – Addition, subtraction, multiplication and division
• *Divide numbers up to 4 digits by a two-digit whole number using the formal written method of long division, and interpret remainders as whole number remainders, fractions, or by rounding, as appropriate for the context*
• *Divide numbers up to 4 digits by a two-digit number using the formal written method of short division where appropriate, interpreting remainders according to the context.*

Long or short division (3)

Learning objectives
I can use a written method to divide numbers up to 4-digits by a 2-digit number.

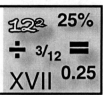

To solve the joke, do the calculation using short or long division. Then use the grid to find the letter that goes with each answer and write it in the speech bubble. The first one has been done for you!

17	59	26	48	35	12	63	24	41	38
B	D	R	L	A	C	I	K	N	O

What falls and never gets hurt?

R _ _ _ _ !

910 ÷ 35 =   1925 ÷ 55 =   693 ÷ 11 =   1845 ÷ 45 =

26
_____   _____   _____   _____

What is black when it's clean and white when it's dirty?

_ _ / _ _ _ _ _ _ _ /

_ _ _ _ _ _ !

1680 ÷ 48

_____

986 ÷ 58 =   864 ÷ 18 =   2520 ÷ 72 =   996 ÷ 83 =   1584 ÷ 66 =

_____   _____   _____   _____   _____

833 ÷ 49 =   2850 ÷ 75 =   3150 ÷ 90 =   962 ÷ 37 =   1888 ÷ 32 =

_____   _____   _____   _____   _____

Year 6 – Addition, subtraction, multiplication and division
- *Divide numbers up to 4 digits by a two-digit whole number using the formal written method of long division, and interpret remainders as whole number remainders, fractions, or by rounding, as appropriate for the context*
- *Divide numbers up to 4 digits by a two-digit number using the formal written method of short division where appropriate, interpreting remainders according to the context.*

Order of operations (1)

Learning objectives
I can solve a calculation with brackets by knowing which order to do the working out.

25%
$\div$ $^{3}/_{12}$
XVII 0.25

To solve the joke, work out the calculation and write the answer in the oval. Then use the grid to find the letter that goes with each answer and write it in the speech bubble. The first one has been done for you!

8	186	32	147	5	153	40	320	96	100	17	45
T	F	A	R	G	E	O	W	I	H	L	S

Which door did the chicken go through to leave the room?

T _ _ _ / _ _ _ _ _ - _ _ _ !

$96 \div (65 - 53) =$

8

$(9 \times 5) + 55 =$

$(30 \times 5) + 3 =$

$(40 \times 4) - 7 =$

$65 \div (10 + 3) =$

$(90 \div 6) \div 3 =$

$130 - (28 + 57) =$

$(4 \times 8) \times 3 =$

$72 - (8 \times 8) =$

Year 6 – Addition, subtraction, multiplication and division
• *Use their knowledge of the order of operations to carry out calculations involving the four operations.*

Order of operations (2)

Learning objectives
I can solve a calculation with brackets by knowing which order to do the working out.

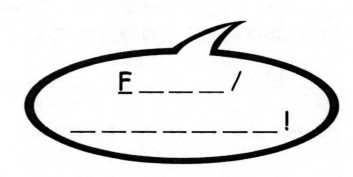

To solve the joke, work out the calculation and write the answer in the oval. Then use the grid to find the letter that goes with each answer and write it in the speech bubble. The first one has been done for you!

8	186	32	147	5	153	40	320	96	150	17	45
T	F	A	R	G	E	O	W	I	H	L	S

What do you call it when it rains chickens?

F _ _ _ _ /
_ _ _ _ _ _ _ _ !

36 + (50 x 3) =

186

28 + (108 ÷ 9) =

350 − (120 ÷ 4) =

170 ÷ (57 − 47) =

(5 x 8) x (72 ÷ 9) =

48 + (6 x 7) + 63 =

(96 ÷ 12) x (12 ÷ 3) =

(57 + 15) ÷ 9 =

81 + (23 x 3) =

200 − (94 ÷ 2) =

171 − (4 x 6) =

Year 6 – Addition, subtraction, multiplication and division
- *Use their knowledge of the order of operations to carry out calculations involving the four operations.*

Order of operations (3)

Learning objectives
I can solve a calculation with brackets by knowing which order to do the working out.

123 25%
÷ 3/12 =
XVII 0.25

To solve the jokes, work out the calculation and write the answer on the line. Then use the grid to find the letter that goes with each answer and write it in the speech bubble. The first one has been done for you!

18	56	29	34	19	111	104	100	147	84	28
O	S	N	T	A	H	C	E	W	M	R

Where did the cow astronaut go?

T _ _ _ / _ _ _ _ _ !

$(87 + 15) \div 3 =$

34

$(6 \times 8) + (9 \times 7) =$

_____

$82 - (5 \times 6) + 48 =$

_____

$12 \times (49 \div 7) =$

_____

$77 - (83 - 24) =$

_____

$3 \times (104 - 98) =$

_____

$85 - (8 \times 7) =$

_____

$(28 + 67) \div (35 \div 7) =$

What is a cow's favourite vegetable?

_ / _ _ _ _ _ _ !

$(4 \times 8) + (12 \times 6) =$

_____

$3 + (49 \div 7) + 8 =$

_____

$(105 \div 5) \times (42 \div 6) =$

_____

$(23 + 31) \div (9 \div 3) =$

_____

$98 - (4 \times 7) - 36 =$

_____

Year 6 – Addition, subtraction, multiplication and division
- *Use their knowledge of the order of operations to carry out calculations involving the four operations.*

Simplifying fractions (1)

123 25%
÷ 3/12 =
XVII 0.25

To solve the joke, reduce each fraction to its simplest form and write the answer in the circle.
Then use the grid to find the letter that goes with each answer and write it in the speech bubble.
The first one is done for you!

$2/9$	$1/2$	$2/5$	$1/4$	$3/11$	$3/7$	$1/3$	$5/8$	$3/4$	$2/3$	$4/5$	$3/8$
I	E	P	R	U	F	Y	N	L	O	A	G

$5/6$	$1/6$	$3/5$	$1/7$	$1/8$
T	C	S	D	M

What kind of plates do astronauts use?

F _ _ _ _ _ _ _ / _ _ _ _ _ _ _ _ !

$6/14$ ($3/7$) $9/12$ ◯ $4/12$ ◯ $6/27$ ◯ $15/24$ ◯ $9/24$ ◯

$12/20$ ◯ $8/10$ ◯ $9/33$ ◯ $2/12$ ◯ $5/10$ ◯ $4/16$ ◯ $15/25$ ◯

Year 6 – Fractions (including decimals and percentages)
• *Use common factors to simplify fractions.*

Simplifying fractions (2)

Learning objectives
I can simplify a fraction by looking for common factors.

123 25%
÷ 3/12 =
XVII 0.25

To solve the joke, reduce each fraction to its simplest form and write the answer in the circle.
Then use the grid to find the letter that goes with each answer and write it in the speech bubble.
The first one is done for you!

2/9	1/2	2/5	1/4	3/11	3/7	1/3	5/8	3/4	2/3	4/5	3/8
I	E	P	R	U	F	Y	N	L	O	A	G

5/6	1/6	3/5	1/7	1/8
T	C	S	D	M

What did the asteroid say to the comet?

P _ _ _ _ _ _ _ / _ _ / _ _ _ _ _ _ _ !

6/15 (**2/5**)   6/8 ( )   3/6 ( )   16/20 ( )   6/10 ( )   10/20 ( )   2/14 ( )

15/18 ( )   4/6 ( )

2/16 ( )   2/4 ( )   20/24 ( )   6/12 ( )   10/15 ( )   3/12 ( )

Year 6 – Fractions (including decimals and percentages)
• *Use common factors to simplify fractions.*

Simplifying fractions (3)

Learning objectives
I can simplify a fraction by looking for common factors.

122 25%
÷ 3/12 =
XVII 0.25

To solve the joke, reduce each fraction to its simplest form and write the answer in the circle.
Then use the grid to find the letter that goes with each answer and write it in the speech bubble.
The first one is done for you!

$3/4$	$2/3$	$4/5$	$3/8$	$5/6$	$1/6$	$3/5$	$1/7$	$1/8$	$2/9$	$1/2$	$2/5$
T	A	R	F	U	S	K	W	L	I	Y	M

$1/4$	$3/11$	$4/7$	$1/3$	$5/8$
E	N	P	G	H

What do you get if you cross an elephant and a fish?

S _ _ _ _ _ _ _ _ / _ _ _ _ _ _ !

$2/12$ (**1/6**) $3/21$ ◯ $8/36$ ◯ $10/25$ ◯ $16/40$ ◯ $10/45$ ◯ $12/44$ ◯ $5/15$ ◯

$18/24$ ◯ $40/50$ ◯ $30/36$ ◯ $15/55$ ◯ $21/35$ ◯ $7/42$ ◯

Year 6 – Fractions (including decimals and percentages)
• *Use common factors to simplify fractions.*

Simplifying fractions (4)

Learning objectives
I can simplify a fraction by looking for common factors.

To solve the joke, reduce each fraction to its simplest form and write the answer in the circle.
Then use the grid to find the letter that goes with each answer and write it in the speech bubble.
The first one is done for you!

3/4	2/3	4/5	3/8	5/6	1/6	3/5	1/7	1/8	2/9	1/2	2/5
T	A	R	F	U	S	K	W	L	I	Y	M

1/4	3/11	4/7	1/3	5/8
E	N	P	G	H

Speech bubble: What looks like an elephant and can fly?

A / _ _ _ _ _ _ / _ _ _ _ _ _ _ !

18/27 (2/3)

21/56 ◯   4/32 ◯   8/16 ◯   16/72 ◯   18/66 ◯   7/21 ◯

11/44 ◯   9/72 ◯   8/32 ◯   28/49 ◯   30/48 ◯   12/18 ◯   21/77 ◯   24/32 ◯

Year 6 – Fractions (including decimals and percentages)
• Use common factors to simplify fractions.

Ordering fractions (1)

Learning objectives
I can compare fractions by finding common factors of multiples of the denominators.
I can compare fractions greater than 1.

122 25%
÷ 3/12 =
XVII 0.25

To solve the jokes, work out which is the largest fraction. Write the answer in the oval, then use the grid to find the letter that goes with each answer and write it in the speech bubble. The first one is done for you!

3/10	1 1/7	1 5/6	2/5	1 4/5	1 7/9	8/12	1 3/8	7/8	5/7	1 1/2	1/9	2/6	1 4/10
E	M	A	W	C	I	R	N	O	G	B	L	T	S

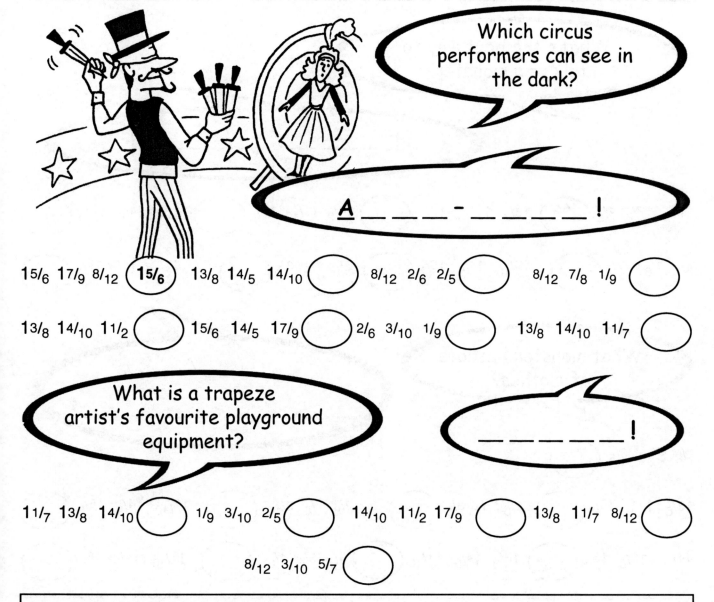

Which circus performers can see in the dark?

A _ _ _ _ - _ _ _ _ _ !

1 5/6 1 7/9 8/12 (1 5/6) 1 3/8 1 4/5 1 4/10 ( ) 8/12 2/6 2/5 ( ) 8/12 7/8 1/9 ( )

1 3/8 1 4/10 1 1/2 ( ) 1 5/6 1 4/5 1 7/9 ( ) 2/6 3/10 1/9 ( ) 1 3/8 1 4/10 1 1/7 ( )

What is a trapeze artist's favourite playground equipment?

_ _ _ _ _ _ !

1 1/7 1 3/8 1 4/10 ( ) 1/9 3/10 2/5 ( ) 1 4/10 1 1/2 1 7/9 ( ) 1 3/8 1 1/7 8/12 ( )

8/12 3/10 5/7 ( )

Year 6 – Fractions (including decimals and percentages)
*   *Use common multiples to express fractions in the same denomination*
*   *Compare and order fractions, including fractions > 1.*

Ordering fractions (2)

Learning objectives
I can compare fractions by finding common factors or multiples of the denominators.
I can compare fractions greater than 1.

122 25%
÷ 3/12 =
XVII 0.25

To solve the jokes, work out which is the largest fraction. Write the answer in the circle, then use the grid to find the letter that goes with each answer and write it in the speech bubble. The first one is done for you!

$2/10$	$12/8$	$16/7$	$3/5$	$15/8$	$17/10$	$3/4$	$13/6$	$7/8$	$4/7$	$11/10$	$1/8$	$2/5$	$14/9$
S	P	F	L	W	R	E	M	A	G	N	Q	U	O

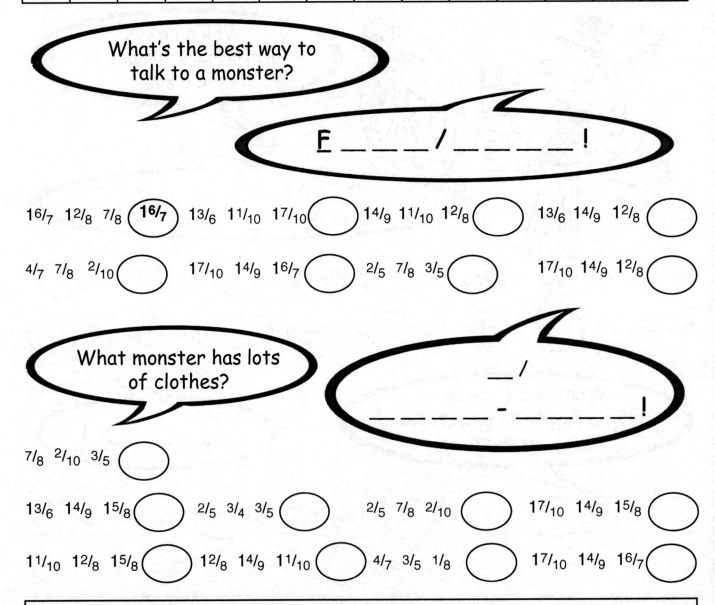

What's the best way to talk to a monster?

F _ _ _ _ / _ _ _ _ _ !

$16/7$ $12/8$ $7/8$ ($\mathbf{16/7}$) $13/6$ $11/10$ $17/10$ ◯ $14/9$ $11/10$ $12/8$ ◯ $13/6$ $14/9$ $12/8$ ◯

$4/7$ $7/8$ $2/10$ ◯ $17/10$ $14/9$ $16/7$ ◯ $2/5$ $7/8$ $3/5$ ◯ $17/10$ $14/9$ $12/8$ ◯

What monster has lots of clothes?

_ /
_ _ _ _ _ - _ _ _ _ !

$7/8$ $2/10$ $3/5$ ◯

$13/6$ $14/9$ $15/8$ ◯ $2/5$ $3/4$ $3/5$ ◯ $2/5$ $7/8$ $2/10$ ◯ $17/10$ $14/9$ $15/8$ ◯

$11/10$ $12/8$ $15/8$ ◯ $12/8$ $14/9$ $11/10$ ◯ $4/7$ $3/5$ $1/8$ ◯ $17/10$ $14/9$ $16/7$ ◯

Year 6 – Fractions (including decimals and percentages)
- *Use common multiples to express fractions in the same denomination*
- *Compare and order fractions, including fractions > 1.*

Adding and subtracting fractions (1)

Learning objectives
I can add and subtract fractions with different denominators.
I can add and subtract mixed numbers.
I can use my knowledge of equivalent fractions.

122 25%
÷ 3/12 =
XVII 0.25

To solve the jokes, work out the answer to the fractions question. Write the answer in the circle, then use the grid to find the letter that goes with each answer and write it in the speech bubble. The first one is done for you!

$1\tfrac{2}{5}$	$\tfrac{7}{9}$	$\tfrac{5}{8}$	$1\tfrac{4}{9}$	$\tfrac{3}{4}$	$1\tfrac{5}{6}$	$\tfrac{2}{5}$	$\tfrac{7}{8}$	$\tfrac{2}{3}$
R	M	O	B	S	F	T	A	E

What did the chicken say when it was learning a new language?

M _ _ _ !

$\tfrac{1}{9} + \tfrac{2}{3} = \left(\tfrac{7}{9}\right)$ 　　 $\tfrac{1}{2} + \tfrac{1}{8} = \bigcirc$ 　　 $\tfrac{3}{4} - \tfrac{1}{8} = \bigcirc$

What do you get if you cross a chicken with a cow?

_ _ _ _ _ _ _ /
_ _ _ _ _ !

$\tfrac{8}{10} + \tfrac{3}{5} = \bigcirc$ 　 $\tfrac{2}{4} + \tfrac{1}{8} = \bigcirc$ 　 $1\tfrac{1}{4} - \tfrac{5}{8} = \bigcirc$ 　 $\tfrac{2}{8} + \tfrac{1}{2} = \bigcirc$ 　 $\tfrac{8}{10} - \tfrac{2}{5} = \bigcirc$

$\tfrac{1}{3} + 1\tfrac{1}{9} = \bigcirc$ 　 $1\tfrac{1}{6} - \tfrac{1}{2} = \bigcirc$ 　 $\tfrac{1}{2} + \tfrac{1}{6} = \bigcirc$ 　 $1\tfrac{1}{3} + \tfrac{1}{2} = \bigcirc$

Year 6 – Fractions (including decimals and percentages)
* *Add and subtract fractions with different denominators and mixed numbers, using the concept of equivalent fractions.*

Adding and subtracting fractions (2)

Learning objectives
I can add and subtract fractions with different denominators.
I can add and subtract mixed numbers.
I can use my knowledge of equivalent fractions.

To solve the jokes, work out the answer to the fractions question. Write the answer in the circle, then use the grid to find the letter that goes with each answer and write it in the speech bubble. The first one is done for you!

$1\frac{3}{5}$	$\frac{8}{9}$	$\frac{7}{8}$	$1\frac{2}{9}$	$\frac{3}{4}$	$1\frac{1}{6}$	$\frac{5}{6}$	$\frac{1}{3}$	$\frac{2}{5}$
L	A	S	G	M	H	B	O	U

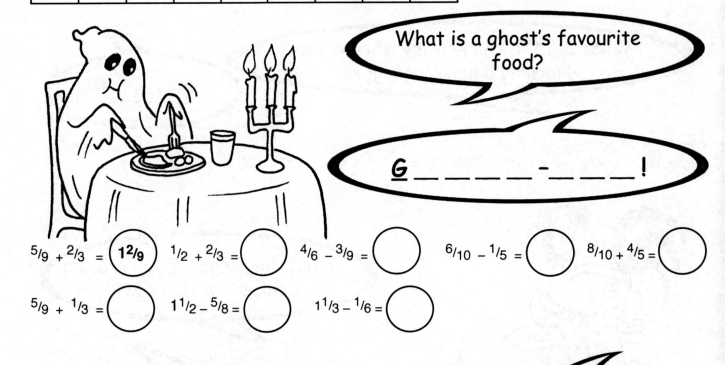

What is a ghost's favourite food?

G _ _ _ _ _ - _ _ _ _ !

$\frac{5}{9} + \frac{2}{3} =$ $1\frac{2}{9}$ $\frac{1}{2} + \frac{2}{3} = \bigcirc$ $\frac{4}{6} - \frac{3}{9} = \bigcirc$ $\frac{6}{10} - \frac{1}{5} = \bigcirc$ $\frac{8}{10} + \frac{4}{5} = \bigcirc$

$\frac{5}{9} + \frac{1}{3} = \bigcirc$ $1\frac{1}{2} - \frac{5}{8} = \bigcirc$ $1\frac{1}{3} - \frac{1}{6} = \bigcirc$

What do ghosts use to wash their hair?

_ _ _ _ _ -
_ _ _ _ _ !

$\frac{1}{8} + \frac{3}{4} = \bigcirc$ $\frac{1}{2} + \frac{2}{3} = \bigcirc$ $1\frac{1}{3} - \frac{4}{9} = \bigcirc$ $1\frac{1}{2} - \frac{6}{8} = \bigcirc$

$\frac{1}{6} + \frac{2}{3} = \bigcirc$ $1\frac{4}{6} - 1\frac{3}{9} = \bigcirc$ $1\frac{2}{3} - 1\frac{2}{6} = \bigcirc$

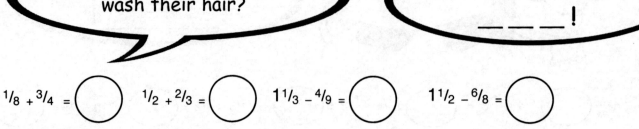

Year 6 – Fractions (including decimals and percentages)
- *Add and subtract fractions with different denominators and mixed numbers, using the concept of equivalent fractions.*

Multiplying fractions (1)

Learning objectives
I can multiply two fractions.
I can simplify fractions and write them in their simplest form.

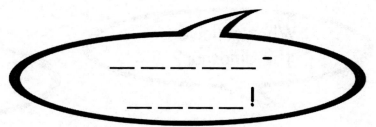

To solve the jokes, work out the answer to the fractions question. Write the answer in the circle, then use the grid to find the letter that goes with each answer and write it in the speech bubble. The first one is done for you!

$2/5$	$2/9$	$1/8$	$3/4$	$1/7$	$1/9$	$2/7$	$5/8$	$1/4$	$1/6$	$1/10$	$3/8$	$1/3$
T	M	N	A	B	U	S	O	I	R	G	E	H

What type of horses only go out when it's dark?

$\underline{N}$ _ _ _ _ - _ _ _ _ _ !

$1/4 \times 1/2 = \left(\textbf{1/8} \right)$ $1/2 \times 1/2 = \bigcirc$ $1/5 \times 1/2 = \bigcirc$ $1/3 \times 3/3 = \bigcirc$ $2/5 \times 2/2 = \bigcirc$

$1/3 \times 2/3 = \bigcirc$ $3/4 \times 4/4 = \bigcirc$ $1/2 \times 2/6 = \bigcirc$ $2/4 \times 3/4 = \bigcirc$ $3/7 \times 2/3 = \bigcirc$

What do you call a horse who lives next door?

_ _ _ _ _ _ -
_ _ _ _ _ !

$2/8 \times 5/10 = \bigcirc$ $1/2 \times 6/8 = \bigcirc$ $2/3 \times 3/8 = \bigcirc$ $3/5 \times 1/6 = \bigcirc$ $1/2 \times 6/9 = \bigcirc$

$2/6 \times 3/7 = \bigcirc$ $5/7 \times 7/8 = \bigcirc$ $2/6 \times 3/9 = \bigcirc$ $1/3 \times 2/4 = \bigcirc$

Year 6 – Fractions (including decimals and percentages)
- *Multiply simple pairs of proper fractions, writing the answer in its simplest form (for example, 1/4 x 1/2 = 1/8).*

Multiplying fractions (2)

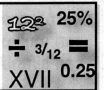

25%

XVII 0.25

To solve the jokes, work out the answer to the fractions question. Write the answer in the circle, then use the grid to find the letter that goes with each answer and write it in the speech bubble. The first one is done for you!

$1/5$	$1/8$	$3/10$	$1/7$	$1/9$	$2/7$	$1/4$	$1/6$	$1/10$	$3/8$
L	D	T	I	E	N	O	R	S	A

What do you call a sleeping dinosaur?

D _ _ _ _ - _ _ _ _ _ _ !

$1/4 \times 4/8 =$ ◯

$4/7 \times 1/4 =$ ◯

$4/7 \times 1/2 =$ ◯

$2/3 \times 3/8 =$ ◯

$3/5 \times 1/6 =$ ◯

$2/5 \times 5/7 =$ ◯

$5/8 \times 2/5 =$ ◯

$1/3 \times 1/2 =$ ◯

$2/9 \times 1/2 =$ ◯

What followed the dinosaur?

_ _ _ _ /

_ _ _ _ !

$2/7 \times 1/2 =$ ◯

$3/5 \times 1/2 =$ ◯

$1/4 \times 2/5 =$ ◯

$3/4 \times 2/5 =$ ◯

$1/2 \times 3/4 =$ ◯

$3/7 \times 1/3 =$ ◯

$1/3 \times 3/5 =$ ◯

Year 6 – Fractions (including decimals and percentages)
* *Multiply simple pairs of proper fractions, writing the answer in its simplest form (for example, 1/4 x 1/2 = 1/8).*

Dividing fractions (1)

Learning objectives
I can divide a proper fraction by a whole number.

123 25%
÷ 3/12 =
XVII 0.25

To solve the jokes, work out the answer to the fractions question. Write the answer in the circle, then use the grid to find the letter that goes with each answer and write it in the speech bubble. The first one is done for you!

2/9	3/8	1/12	1/8	3/10	5/12	1/9	2/15	1/4	1/6	1/10	1/15
D	A	S	N	O	E	T	H	U	I	R	G

$1/3 \div 4 =$ (**1/12**) $1/3 \div 3 =$ ◯

$1/2 \div 2 =$ ◯ $1/5 \div 2 =$ ◯

$1/5 \div 3 =$ ◯ $5/6 \div 2 =$ ◯

$3/5 \div 2 =$ ◯ $1/2 \div 4 =$ ◯

$1/2 \div 6 =$ ◯

What type of fish work in hospitals?

S _ _ _ _ _ _ _ _ _ _ !

What type of fish help you to hear better?

_ _ _ _ _ _ _ _ _ /
_ _ _ _ _ !

$2/3 \div 5 =$ ◯ $5/6 \div 2 =$ ◯ $1/5 \div 2 =$ ◯ $1/2 \div 5 =$ ◯ $1/2 \div 3 =$ ◯

$1/4 \div 2 =$ ◯ $1/3 \div 5 =$ ◯

$3/4 \div 2 =$ ◯ $1/3 \div 2 =$ ◯ $2/3 \div 3 =$ ◯ $1/6 \div 2 =$ ◯

Year 6 – Fractions (including decimals and percentages)
• *Divide proper fractions by whole numbers (for example 1/3 ÷ 2 = 1/6).*

Dividing fractions (2)

Learning objectives
I can divide a proper fraction by a whole number.

To solve the jokes, work out the answer to the fractions question. Write the answer in the circle, then use the grid to find the letter that goes with each answer and write it in the speech bubble. The first one is done for you!

$3/8$	$1/12$	$1/8$	$1/4$	$1/9$	$2/9$	$3/10$	$1/6$	$1/15$
E	C	T	A	S	O	R	I	K

What is brown and sticky?

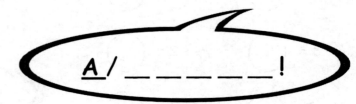

A / _ _ _ _ _ _ !

$1/2 \div 2 =$ ($1/4$)

$1/3 \div 3 =$ ◯ $1/2 \div 4 =$ ◯ $1/3 \div 2 =$ ◯ $1/4 \div 3 =$ ◯ $1/3 \div 5 =$ ◯

How do you get a baby to sleep in space?

_ _ _ _ _ / _ _ !

$3/5 \div 2 =$ ◯ $2/3 \div 3 =$ ◯ $1/6 \div 2 =$ ◯ $1/5 \div 3 =$ ◯

$1/2 \div 3 =$ ◯ $1/4 \div 2 =$ ◯

Year 6 – Fractions (including decimals and percentages)
* *Divide proper fractions by whole numbers (for example 1/3 ÷ 2 = 1/6).*

Decimal fraction equivalents (1)

To solve the jokes, use division to convert each fraction to a decimal. Write the answer in the ovals, then use the grid to find the letter that goes with each answer and write it in the speech bubble. The first one is done for you!

0.375	0.125	0.75	0.625	0.7	0.8	0.15	0.25	0.2	0.3	0.875	0.05	0.4
T	D	H	O	Q	E	U	S	A	W	C	N	K

What did the detective duck want to do?

Q_ _ _ _ _ _ / _ _ _ _ / _ _ _ _ _ !

$14/20$ **0.7** $3/20$ ( ) $4/20$ ( ) $7/8$ ( ) $6/15$ ( )

$3/8$ ( ) $9/12$ ( ) $4/5$ ( )

$7/8$ ( ) $2/10$ ( ) $3/12$ ( ) $8/10$ ( )

What direction do ducks' feathers grow in?

_ _ _ _ _ !

$1/8$ ( ) $5/8$ ( ) $6/20$ ( ) $1/20$ ( )

Decimal fraction equivalents (2)

Learning objectives
I can connect fractions with division to calculate the decimal equivalents of simple fractions.

To solve the jokes, use division to convert each fraction to a decimal. Write the answer in the ovals, then use the grid to find the letter that goes with each answer and write it in the speech bubble. The first one is done for you!

0.375	0.125	0.75	0.625	0.45	0.8	0.15	0.2	0.35	0.875	0.4
G	R	S	K	C	T	A	F	I	E	N

What is a vampire's favourite fruit?

N___ ___ - ___ ___ ___ ___ ___ ___ ___!

$6/15$ (0.4) $7/8$ ◯ $9/20$ ◯ $5/8$ ◯

$4/5$ ◯ $3/20$ ◯ $1/8$ ◯ $7/20$ ◯

$6/15$ ◯ $7/8$ ◯ $9/12$ ◯

What is a vampire's favourite animal?

___ / ___ ___ ___ ___ ___ ___ ___!

$3/20$ ◯ $3/8$ ◯ $7/20$ ◯ $1/8$ ◯

$3/20$ ◯ $3/15$ ◯ $4/20$ ◯ $7/8$ ◯

Year 6 – Fractions (including decimals and percentages)
• *Associate a fraction with division and calculate decimal fraction equivalents; for example, 0.375 for a simple fraction 3/8.*

Place value of decimals (1)

Learning objectives
I know the value of each digit in numbers with three decimal places.
I can use place value to multiply and divide numbers by 10, 100 or
    1000 with answers up to 3 decimal places.

To solve the jokes, use place value to work out the value of the underlined digit and write the answer in the ovals. Then use the grid to find the letter that goes with each answer and write it in the speech bubble. The first one is done for you!

0.02	0.2	0.9	0.005	0.009	0.06	0.05	0.6
L	S	E	R	A	T	P	Y

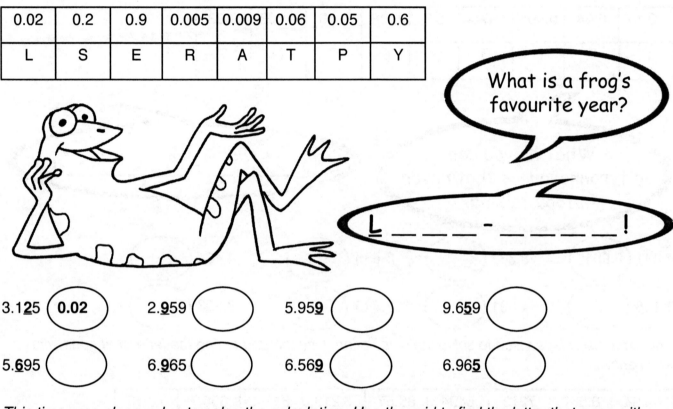

What is a frog's favourite year?

L _ _ _ _ - _ _ _ _ !

3.1<u>2</u>5 (0.02)   2.<u>9</u>59 ( )   5.95<u>9</u> ( )   9.6<u>5</u>9 ( )

5.<u>6</u>95 ( )   6.<u>9</u>65 ( )   6.56<u>9</u> ( )   6.96<u>5</u> ( )

This time, use place value to solve the calculation. Use the grid to find the letter that goes with each answer.

52.25	21.23	2.123	5.225	522.5	2123
M	L	C	I	E	Y

What do you call a girl with a frog on her head?

_ _ _ _ _ !

2.123 x 10 = ( )   5225 ÷ 1000 = ( )   2123 ÷ 100 = ( )   2.123 x 1000 = ( )

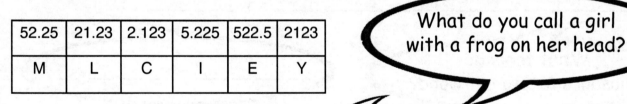

Year 6 – Fractions (including decimals and percentages)
- *Identify the value of each digit in numbers given to three decimal places and multiply and divide numbers by 10, 100 and 1000 giving answers up to three decimal places.*

Place value of decimals (2)

Learning objectives
I know the value of each digit in numbers with three decimal places.
I can use place value to multiply and divide numbers by 10, 100 or
   1000 with answers up to 3 decimal places.

122   25%
÷ 3/12 =
XVII 0.25

To solve the first jokes, use place value to work out the value of the underlined digit and write the answer in the oval. Then use the grid to find the letter that goes with each answer and write it in the speech bubble. The first one is done for you!

0.1	0.04	0.001	0.004	0.3	0.08	0.03	0.008	0.003
S	R	D	B	I	E	O	N	T

What do you call
a tyrannosaurus that never
stops talking?

<u>D</u> _ _ _ _ - _ _ _ _ _ !

4.33<u>1</u> (0.001)   8.<u>3</u>83 ( )   8.43<u>8</u> ( )   4.4<u>3</u>4 ( )

3.14<u>4</u> ( )   4.8<u>3</u>1 ( )   3.8<u>4</u>3 ( )   8.3<u>8</u>3 ( )

This time, use place value to solve the calculation. Use the grid to find the letter that goes with each answer.

64.94	8.557	7213	6494	85.57	7.213	649.4	855.7	72.13
L	D	T	I	W	N	A	S	O

What tools do
dinosaurs use to cut wood?

_ _ _ _ _ - _ _ _ _ _ !

8557 ÷ 1000 = ( )   6.494 x 1000 = ( )   721.3 ÷ 100 = ( )   7.213 x 10 = ( )

8.557 x 100 = ( )   6494 ÷ 10 = ( )   8557 ÷ 100 = ( )   8.557 x 100 = ( )

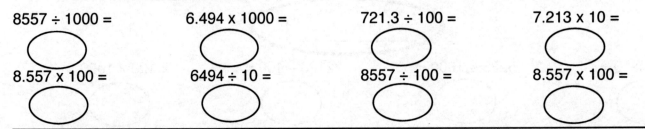

Year 6 – Fractions (including decimals and percentages)
* *Identify the value of each digit in numbers given to three decimal places and multiply and divide numbers by 10, 100 and 1000 giving answers up to three decimal places.*

Multiplying decimals (1)

Learning objectives
I can multiply a one-digit number with up to two decimal places by
a whole number.

To solve the jokes, work out the answer to the calculation and write it in the oval. Then use the grid to find the letter that goes with each answer and write it in the speech bubble. The first one is done for you!

18.8	40.6	14.4	13.58	59.22	31.9	22.92	56.7	52.2	9.4	43.2	27	9.84
L	K	T	U	H	S	E	M	B	R	A	O	C

What should you do when teachers roll their eyes at you?

R _ _ _ _ _ / _ _ _ _ _ / _ _ _ _ _ !

2.35 x 4 = (9.4)   4.5 x 6 = ( )   3.76 x 5 = ( )   4.7 x 4 = ( )

3.6 x 4 = ( )   8.46 x 7 = ( )   5.73 x 4 = ( )   6.3 x 9 = ( )

8.7 x 6 = ( )   5.4 x 8 = ( )   3.28 x 3 = ( )   5.8 x 7 = ( )

How do you get straight A's in school?

_ _ _ _ / _ _ /
_ _ _ _ _ _ !

1.94 x 7 = ( )   6.38 x 5 = ( )   3.82 x 6 = ( )   4.8 x 9 = ( )

1.88 x 5 = ( )   6.79 x 2 = ( )   2.35 x 8 = ( )   3.82 x 6 = ( )   4.7 x 2 = ( )

Year 6 – Fractions (including decimals and percentages)
- *Multiply one-digit numbers with up to two decimal places by whole numbers.*

Multiplying decimals (2)

Learning objectives
I can multiply a one-digit number with up to two decimal places by a whole number.

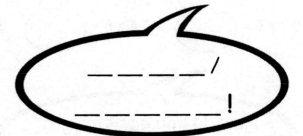

25%
÷ 3/12 =
XVII 0.25

To solve the jokes, work out the answer to the calculation and write it in the oval. Then use the grid to find the letter that goes with each answer and write it in the speech bubble. The first one is done for you!

76	74.07	24.3	27.28	44.1	22.96	40.6	35.6	28
L	F	A	T	S	O	P	W	E

What gets wetter the more it dries?

A / _ _ _ _ _ _ !

2.7 x 9 = (**24.3**)

3.41 x 8 = ◯   3.28 x 7 = ◯   8.9 x 4 = ◯   3.5 x 8 = ◯   9.5 x 8 = ◯

The more you take of me, the more you leave behind. What am I?

_ _ _ _ _ /
_ _ _ _ _ _ !

8.23 x 9 = ◯   2.87 x 8 = ◯   5.74 x 4 = ◯   6.82 x 4 = ◯

6.3 x 7 = ◯   13.64 x 2 = ◯   5.6 x 5 = ◯   5.8 x 7 = ◯   8.82 x 5 = ◯

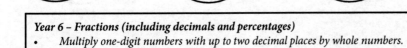

Year 6 – Fractions (including decimals and percentages)
- *Multiply one-digit numbers with up to two decimal places by whole numbers.*

Division of decimals (1)

Learning objectives
I can divide a number with up to two decimal places by a whole number, with answers up to two decimal places.

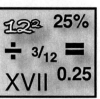

To solve the jokes, work out the answer to the calculation and write it in the oval. Then use the grid to find the letter that goes with each answer and write it in the speech bubble. The first one is done for you!

3.06	3.28	0.47	1.09	2.58	1.58	1.03	1.06	2.4	2.05
T	O	U	H	A	P	Y	D	E	N

How did the frog feel when he broke his leg?

U _ / _ _ _ _ _ _ !

2.35 ÷ 5 = (**0.47**)   8.2 ÷ 4 = ( )

6.54 ÷ 6 = ( )   9.84 ÷ 3 = ( )   6.32 ÷ 4 = ( )   9.48 ÷ 6 = ( )   7.21 ÷ 7 = ( )

What type of shoes does a frog wear?

_ _ _ _ _ /
_ _ _ _ _ !

6.56 ÷ 2 = ( )   7.9 ÷ 5 = ( )   9.6 ÷ 4 = ( )   6.15 ÷ 3 = ( )

9.18 ÷ 3 = ( )   13.12 ÷ 4 = ( )   12.9 ÷ 5 = ( )   9.54 ÷ 9 = ( )

Year 6 – Fractions (including decimals and percentages)
* *Use written division methods in cases where the answer has up to two decimal places.*

Division of decimals (2)

Learning objectives
I can divide a number with up to two decimal places by a whole number, with answers up to two decimal places.

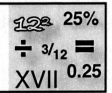

To solve the jokes, work out the answer to the calculation and write it in the oval. Then use the grid to find the letter that goes with each answer and write it in the speech bubble. The first one is done for you!

1.29	1.9	1.6	2.6	0.43	1.35	1.62	2.09	2.13	3.5	0.52	0.66
S	B	G	H	I	N	C	D	A	F	K	E

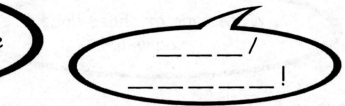

What do fish have on their birthdays?

$10.5 \div 3 =$ (**3.5**) $2.58 \div 6 =$ ( )

$3.87 \div 3 =$ ( ) $10.4 \div 4 =$ ( )

F _ _ _ _ / _ _ _ _ _ _ !

$8.1 \div 5 =$ ( ) $8.52 \div 4 =$ ( ) $3.64 \div 7 =$ ( ) $5.94 \div 9 =$ ( ) $5.16 \div 4 =$ ( )

If you have 6 oranges in one hand and 7 oranges in the other, what do you have?

_ _ _ _ / _ _ _ _ _ _ !

$15.2 \div 8 =$ ( ) $3.01 \div 7 =$ ( ) $8 \div 5 =$ ( )

$7.8 \div 3 =$ ( ) $6.39 \div 3 =$ ( ) $8.1 \div 6 =$ ( ) $8.36 \div 4 =$ ( ) $6.45 \div 5 =$ ( )

Year 6 – Fractions (including decimals and percentages)
*   *Use written division methods in cases where the answer has up to two decimal places.*

Answers

Year 5
Place value and ordering

Activity 1	300; 300,000; 5000; 5000; 800,000; 3000; 5000; 900,000; 30,000	A BOOK WORM!	5
	865,309; 125 806; 354,543; 865,093	BUGS!	
Activity 2	20,000; 600,000; 2000; 6000; 40,000; 400; 600,000; 400,000; 200,000	MORSE TOAD!	6
Activity 3	658,123; 658,321; 659,112; 444,518; 443,518; 443,158; 443,158; 443,185; 658,321; 981,891; 982,981; 981,981	KERMIT THE FOG!	7

Sequences in powers of 10

Activity 1	982,235; 790,750; 360,225; 981,901; 364,005; 9111; 10,111; 303,905	LEAP FROG!	8
Activity 2	980,950; 9111; 10,111; 360,225; 789,750; 799,750; 899,079	CROAK-US!	9
Activity 3	199,805; 690,500; 489,805; 109,805; 605,905; 139,139; 149,149; 500,805	OWL-GEBRA!	10
	500,805; 109,805; 149,149; 199,805; 690,500; 489,805	A GROWL!	

Negative numbers

Activity 1	-5, -9, -1, -4, -15, -16, -10, -15, -8, -2, -2, -9	PLAICE SCHOOL!	11
	-15, -2, -6	COD!	
Activity 2	-4, -15, -8, -16, -5, -9, -10, -1, -15	NEW YORKIE!	12
	-2, -5, -5, -6, -7, -15, -20	POODLES!	

Rounding to 10, 100, 1000, 10,000 and 100,000

Activity 1	550,000; 555,550; 500,000; 504,400; 504,000	STUCK!	13
	600,000; 400,400; 555,550; 550,000; 400,400;		
	505,000; 400,500; 400,400, 400,400, 450,000	LOTS OF ROOM!	
Activity 2	890,000; 800,000; 800,900; 908,000; 980,000;		
	900,800; 908,000; 809,000; 808,000	QUIET PEAS!	14
	809,000; 900,000; 908,000; 908,000; 890,890	A LEEK!	

Roman numerals

Activity 1	39, 594, 975, 999, 159, 975, 400, 107, 243, 975	THE APE VINE!	15
	1454, 1992, 1454, 2009, 2009, 1949	BA-BOOM!	
Activity 2	925, 952, 842, 842, 482, 822, 925, 538, 925, 588	A ROOT CANAL!	16
	1929, 1490, 1490, 1929, 1992, 1940, 2016,		
	1904, 2014	TOOTH PICS!	

Addition and subtraction

Activity 1	456,522; 805,805; 231,225; 456,522; 456,522; 69,826	EILEEN!	17
	952,108; 111,333; 93,502; 231,225; 59,812; 67,488; 93,502; 69,826	A POLYGON	

| Activity 2 | 64,582; 741,258; 985,689; 741,258; 52,858; 985,689; 80,854; 23,508 | A POP SONG! | 18 |
| | 64,582; 20,256; 321,654; 46,452; 46,825 | A DUCK! | |

Prime numbers

Activity 1	7, 19, 79, 53, 67, 89, 37, 53, 23, 47, 89, 37, 53	FRANK EINSTEIN!	19
Activity 2	19, 73, 59, 89, 73, 79, 53, 41, 83, 31, 73, 43, 11, 37, 89, 47	ROMEO AND GHOULIET!	20
Activity 3	29, 83, 37, 59, 59, 79, 83, 67, 17, 17, 5, 7, 59	GLASS FLIPPERS!	21
Activity 4	59, 53, 61, 67, 89, 31, 37, 17, 17, 5, 7, 59	SQUID-NAPPERS!	22

Long multiplication

Activity 1	24,111; 4608; 23,184; 23,184; 24,780; 24,111; 4608; 23,184; 23,184; 24,780	HELLO, HELLO!	23
	132,960; 40,824; 3176; 24,780; 33,966; 40,824; 50,463; 4608	DINO-MITE AN EGG!	24
Activity 2	8346; 35,216; 30,510; 25,784; 25,784		
	7554; 30,510; 28,782; 8346; 29,667; 31,524; 32,562; 30,510	HE'S ALIVE!	

Short division

Activity 1	656.8, $44\frac{1}{2}$, 357r4, 32, 856, 431r2, $724\frac{3}{4}$, 357r4, 155r2, 456r1, 96.25	HERMIT CRABS!	25
Activity 2	$724\frac{3}{4}$, 269, 357r4, 155r2, 87.5, 96.25, 856, 37r6, 352, $44\frac{1}{2}$, 357r4, 96.25	CORAL SINGERS!	26
Activity 3	622.5, 236r3, 657, 137r1, 657, 164.4, 137r1, 856, 622.5	MICE CREAM!	27
Activity 4	622.5, 137r1, $89\frac{1}{2}$, $56\frac{1}{4}$, 229r4, 236r3, 657	MEOW-SIC!	28

x and ÷ whole numbers and decimals by 10, 100 or 1000

Activity 1	0.59, 14.6, 0.035, 1.46, 146, 59, 0.28, 590	VERY LOST!	29
Activity 2	350, 3.5, 2.8, 3.5, 350, 2800, 146, 59, 59	IN AN IGLOO!	30
Activity 3	2400, 580, 30.6, 240, 5.8, 2.4, 3600, 240, 470	MILK SHAKE!	31
Activity 4	30.6, 470, 3600, 0.36, 4700, 470, 470, 360	LEAN BEEF!	32

Square and cube numbers

Activity 1	64, 9, 1, 125, 1, 64, 64, 1, 8, 1	THE LETTER E!	33
	64, 9, 1, 81, 16, 27, 36, 25, 81	THE WINDOW!	
Activity 2	9, 125, 49, 81, 27, 64, 36, 4, 25, 9, 49, 8	A BRIGHT SPARK!	34
Activity 3	4, 8, 64, 27, 81, 64, 8, 36, 125, 144, 64, 8, 49	ON A GIANT'S HAND!	35

Understanding the 'equals' sign

Activity 1	55, 25, 32	SIR!	36
	100, 60, 75, 13, 10, 90, 60, 47	CAT WOMAN!	
Activity 2	5, 40, 6, 8, 6, 27	THE SEA!	37
	27, 10, 30, 50, 18, 6, 15	A MONKEY!	

Compare and order fractions

| Activity 1 | $\frac{7}{9}$, $\frac{3}{8}$, $\frac{5}{8}$, $\frac{7}{9}$, $\frac{6}{10}$, $\frac{5}{6}$, $\frac{4}{5}$, $\frac{8}{12}$, $\frac{7}{8}$ | CHICK PEAS! | 38 |
| | $\frac{7}{14}$, $\frac{8}{12}$, $\frac{8}{9}$, $\frac{8}{9}$, $\frac{5}{6}$, $\frac{1}{4}$, $\frac{5}{8}$, $\frac{3}{3}$, $\frac{4}{10}$, $\frac{3}{8}$, $\frac{4}{5}$, $\frac{3}{3}$, $\frac{7}{8}$ | BALL POINT HENS | |

Improper fractions and mixed numbers

Adding and subtracting fractions

Multiplying fractions

Rounding decimals

Comparing decimals up to 3 places

Fraction decimal and percentage equivalents

Place value and ordering

Activity 2	2,865,309; 2,354,543; 4,125,608; 4,125,806; 2,354,354; 2,865,039	A TRUNK!	57
Activity 3	70,000; 200,000; 4,000,000; 8,000,000; 70,000; 200,000; 4,000,000; 8,000,000	KELP! KELP!	58
Activity 4	3,465,587; 3,258,258; 3,456,889; 3,199,981; 3,258,852; 3,465,578; 3,258,528	DRY ONES!	59

Negative numbers

Activity 1	10, 3, 14, 6, 7, 20, 5, 3	NEST CAFE!	60
Activity 2	8, 15, 0, 2, 10	ROBIN!	61
Activity 3	1, 9, 3, 10, 3, 20, 1, 9	HEAD ACHE	62
	5, 8, 5, 9	NINE	

Long multiplication

Activity 1	67,648; 9150; 155,652; 88,524; 56,126; 25,026; 67,648; 9150; 32,120; 56,126; 56,126; 35,258	THE SOUTH POOL!	63
Activity 2	88,524; 67,648; 40,968; 115,720; 19,305; 41,262; 88,524; 9150	STAR FISH!	64
Activity 3	10,620; 84,640; 340,860; 62,888; 84,640; 4288; 84,640; 612,105	TAKE-AWAY!	65
Activity 4	6554; 91,203; 58,536; 87,560; 62,888; 87,560; 84,640; 107,315; 474,000; 4288; 4579; 9163; 76,084; 62,888; 87,560	MOUSE SANDWICHES	66

Long or short division

Activity 1	28, 35, 35, 12, 35, 16, 35, 25	BAA-HAMAS	67
Activity 2	28, 35, 35, 28, 35, 35, 52, 18, 37, 25	BAA-BAA-CUES	68
Activity 3	26, 35, 63, 41	RAIN!	69
	35, 17, 48, 35, 12, 24, 17, 38, 35, 26, 59	A BLACK BOARD!	

Order of operations

Activity 1	8, 100, 153, 153, 5, 5, 45, 96, 8	THE EGGS-IT!	70
Activity 2	186, 40, 320, 17, 320, 153, 32, 8, 150, 153, 147	FOWL WEATHER!	71
Activity 3	34, 111, 100, 84, 18, 18, 29	THE MOON!	72
	19, 104, 18, 147, 18, 34	A COWOT!	

Simplifyng fractions

Activity 1	$3/7$, $3/4$, $1/3$, $2/9$, $5/8$, $3/8$, $3/5$, $4/5$, $3/11$, $1/6$, $1/2$, $1/4$, $3/5$	FLYING SAUCERS!	73
Activity 2	$2/5$, $3/4$, $1/2$, $4/5$, $3/5$, $1/2$, $1/7$, $5/6$, $2/3$, $1/8$, $1/2$, $5/6$, $1/2$ $2/3$, $1/4$	PLEASED TO METEOR!	74
Activity 3	$1/6$, $1/7$, $2/9$, $2/5$, $2/5$, $2/9$, $3/11$, $1/3$, $3/4$, $4/5$, $5/6$, $3/11$, $3/5$, $1/6$	SWIMMING TRUNKS!	75
Activity 4	$2/3$, $3/8$, $1/8$, $1/2$, $2/9$, $3/11$, $1/3$, $1/4$, $1/8$, $1/4$, $4/7$, $5/8$, $2/3$, $3/11$, $3/4$	A FLYING ELEPHANT!	76

Ordering fractions

| Activity 1 | $1\,5/6$, $1\,4/5$, $8/12$, $7/8$, $1\,1/2$, $1\,5/6$, $2/6$, $1\,4/10$ $1\,4/10$, $2/5$, $1\,7/9$, $1\,3/8$, $5/7$, | ACRO-BATS SWING! | 77 |

Activity 2   1 $6/_7$, 1 $7/_{10}$, 1 $4/_9$, 1 $3/_6$, $7/_8$, 1 $6/_7$, $7/_8$, 1 $7/_{10}$ FROM AFAR!   78
$7/_8$, 1 $5/_8$, $3/_4$, $7/_8$, 1 $7/_{10}$, 1 $5/_8$, 1 $4/_9$, $3/_5$, 1 $6/_7$ A WEAR-WOLF!

Adding and subtractioning fractions

Activity 1 $7/_9$, $5/_8$, $5/_8$ MOO!   79
1 $2/_5$, $5/_8$, $5/_8$, $3/_4$, $2/_5$, 1 $4/_9$, $2/_3$, $2/_3$, 1 $5/_6$ ROOST BEEF!

Activity 2   1 $2/_9$, 1 $1/_6$, $1/_3$, $2/_5$, 1 $3/_5$, $8/_9$, $7/_8$, 1 $1/_6$ GHOUL-ASH!   80
$7/_8$, 1 $1/_6$, $8/_9$, $3/_4$, $5/_6$, $1/_3$, $1/_3$ SHAM-BOO!

Multiplying fractions

Activity 1 $1/_8$, $1/_4$, $1/_{10}$, $1/_3$, $2/_5$, $2/_9$, $3/_4$, $1/_6$, $3/_8$, $2/_7$ NIGHT-MARES!   81
$1/_8$, $3/_8$, $1/_4$, $1/_{10}$, $1/_3$, $1/_7$, $5/_8$, $1/_9$, $1/_6$ NEIGH-BOUR!

Activity 2 $1/_8$, $1/_7$, $2/_7$, $1/_4$, $1/_{10}$, $2/_7$, $1/_4$, $1/_6$, $1/_9$ DINO-SNORE!   82
$1/_7$, $3/_{10}$, $1/_{10}$, $3/_{10}$, $3/_8$, $1/_7$, $1/_5$ ITS TAIL!

Dividing fractions

Activity 1 $1/_{12}$, $1/_9$, $1/_4$, $1/_{10}$, $1/_{15}$, $5/_{12}$, $3/_{10}$, $1/_8$, $1/_{12}$ STURGEONS!   83
$2/_{15}$, $5/_{12}$, $1/_{10}$, $1/_{10}$, $1/_6$, $1/_8$, $1/_{15}$, $3/_8$, $1/_6$, $2/_9$, $1/_{12}$ HERRING AIDS

Activity 2 $1/_4$, $1/_9$, $1/_8$, $1/_6$, $1/_{12}$, $1/_{15}$ A STICK!   84
$3/_{10}$, $2/_9$, $1/_{12}$, $1/_{15}$, $1/_6$, $1/_8$ ROCK IT!

Decimal fraction equivalents

Activity 1   0.7, 0.15, 0.2, 0.875, 0.4, 0.375, 0.75, 0.8, 0.875   QUACK THE
0.2, 0.25, 0.8   CASE!   85
0.125, 0.625, 0.3, 0.05   DOWN!

Activity 2   0.4, 0.875, 0.45, 0.625, 0.8, 0.15, 0.125, 0.35
0.4, 0.875, 0.75   NECK-TARINES!   86
0.15, 0.375, 0.35, 0.125, 0.15, 0.2, 0.2, 0.875   A GIRAFFE!

Place value of decimals

Activity 1   0.02, 0.9, 0.009, 0.05, 0.6, 0.9, 0.009, 0.005   LEAP YEAR!   87
21.23, 5.225, 21.23, 2123   LILY

Activity 2   0.001, 0.3, 0.008, 0.03, 0.004, 0.03, 0.04, 0.08   DINO-BORE!   88
8.557, 6494, 7.213, 72.13, 855.7, 649.4,
85.57, 855.7   DINO-SAWS!

Multiplying decimals

Activity 1   9.4, 27, 18.8, 18.8, 14.4, 59.22, 22.92, 56.7, 52.2,
43.2, 9.84, 40.6   ROLL THEM BACK!   89
13.58, 31.9, 22.92, 43.2, 9.4, 13.58, 18.8,
22.92, 9.4   USE A RULER!

Activity 2   24.3, 27.28, 22.96, 35.6, 28, 76   A TOWEL!   90
74.07, 22.96, 22.96, 27.28, 44.1, 27.28, 28,
40.6, 44.1   FOOT STEPS!

Division of decimals

Activity 1   0.47, 2.05, 1.09, 3.28, 1.58, 1.58, 1.03   UN-HOPPY!   91
3.28, 1.58, 2.4, 2.05, 3.06, 3.28, 2.58, 1.06   OPEN TOAD!

Activity 2   3.5, 0.43, 1.29, 2.6, 1.62, 2.13, 0.52, 0.66, 1.29   FISH CAKES!   92
1.9, 0.43, 1.6, 2.6, 2.13, 1.35, 2.09, 1.29   BIG HANDS!

Assessment checklist

Put a ✔ in the box when the pupil has successfully completed the activity.

Name _____   Class _____

Year 5	1	2	3	4
Place value and ordering				
Sequences in powers of 10				
Negative numbers				
Rounding to 10, 100, 1000, 10,000 and 100,000				
Roman numerals				
Addition and subtraction				
Prime numbers				
Long multiplication				
Short division				
Multiply and divide whole numbers and decimals				
Square and cube numbers				
Understanding the 'equals' sign				
Compare and order fractions				
Improper fractions and mixed numbers				
Adding and subtracting fractions				
Multiplying fractions				
Rounding decimals				
Comparing decimals up to 3 places				
Fraction, decimal and percentage equivalents				

Assessment checklist

Put a ✔ in the box when the pupil has successfully completed the activity.

Name _____   Class _____

Year 6	1	2	3	4
Place, value and ordering				
Negative numbers				
Long multiplication				
Long or short division				
Order of operations				
Simplifying fractions				
Ordering fractions				
Adding and subtracting fractions				
Multiplying fractions				
Dividing fractions				
Decimal fraction equivalents				
Place value of decimals				
Multiplying decimals				
Division of decimals